D1058781

THE CLOCK
AND
THE CALENDAR

A Front-Row Look at the Democrats'
Obsession with Donald Trump

BY DOUG COLLINS

A POST HILL PRESS BOOK
ISBN: 978-1-63758-088-2
ISBN (eBook): 978-1-63758-089-9

The Clock and the Calendar:
A Front-Row Look at the Democrats' Obsession with Donald Trump

Cover Photograph by Hassel Weems

This is a work of nonfiction. All people, locations, events, and situations are portrayed to the best of the author's memory.

Post Hill Press
New York • Nashville
posthillpress.com

Published in the United States of America
1 2 3 4 5 6 7 8 9 10

DEDICATION

I have been able to do many things in my life and this book records a little bit of that journey. However, I am only able to do this because I have the best partner in life that anyone could ask for. Lisa is more than a wife. She is my confidante, sounding board, strength when I am weak, best friend, and most importantly, the love of my life. You are in everything that I do and that includes the words of this book. I also am blessed to be father to Jordan, Copelan, and Cameron. You are the reason that I pursued public service and the reason that I have hope for the future.

TABLE OF CONTENTS

Foreword
A Truth Teller with Integrity

As a journalist, knowing whom to trust is critical. In 2017, Doug Collins was one of a small group of lawmakers who went against the grain and showed tremendous courage and a willingness to be ridiculed and attacked in his commitment to truth. This book will tell you how.

The Clock and the Calendar gives you a direct line into how President Trump's detractors tried to take him down any way they could. When I started covering Washington closely about eight years ago, I had no idea the amount of dirty tricks and corruption that existed. I had come from the worlds of business and media where cutthroat attacks certainly existed, and I did not think anything could compare to the backstabbing that I had seen firsthand. But I was wrong. I would never have imagined that one political campaign could come up with a completely made-up story against their political rival and be successful in rallying U.S. government agencies and the media to go along with it, and in doing so, convince the entire country of a lie. I had no clue about the level some might stoop to undo their political enemies. This is one reason I was so outraged to learn all about the made-up Steele Dossier in 2017 and 2018 and the hysteria that ensued across America about their so-called Trump-Russia collusion story. As a journalist for more than thirty years, I pride myself on my intuition and judgment, and once again it served me well here. I knew whom to listen to. While virtually the entire media landscape was reporting on President Trump colluding against America and some in the FBI, CIA, and State Department were selectively leaking whispers to the media to continue the lie, I knew whom to trust and whom not to trust.

I started talking more to then Georgia Congressman Doug Collins, who was a member of the Judiciary Committee. He is also an attorney and served as a chaplain at the U.S. Air Force Reserve with a rank of lieutenant colonel. He was among the few patriots pushing back against this extraordinary charge that Trump somehow worked with Russia to steal the 2016 election. He and his colleagues demanded evidence of the collusion story. They walked me through how Democrats were leading a charge against Trump and made sure I understood the hypocrisy of certain lawmakers saying one thing behind closed doors and a completely different story while on Trump-hating networks CNN and MSNBC. It was astounding. The made-up dossier, the muddying up and wiretapping of innocent Americans like Carter Page and George Papadopoulos. The use of wiretaps, informants, and doctored evidence against Trump associates, while hiding the real exculpatory evidence the entire time. The leaks from government bureaucrats—one leak a day in President's Trump's first days in office—125 leaks in the first 126 days, 62 of those leaks actually threatened national security. A year earlier, in 2016, Hillary Clinton supporters started circulating a bogus dossier of smears alleging that Trump had been compromised by the Russian government. They got it in front of the FBI and CIA, among other agencies, which did not dispute it, nor did the leadership of those agencies report that the creation of the dossier was actually funded entirely by the Hillary Clinton campaign and the Democratic National Committee during a presidential election year. The campaign hired a law firm and political operatives to build the dossier against Trump. The author of the dossier, Christopher Steele, said his information came from "primary sub sources," who by 2017 told the FBI, under oath, that many of the most sensational claims were simply made "in jest." So the government agencies knew by the time Trump began his presidency that it was all made up. Yet they allowed the speculation to run wild for years to undermine his presidency. They went even further, employing the very surveillance tools usually reserved for terrorists and other foreign enemies against associates of Donald Trump. It would take until December 2019, almost three full years into Trump's presidency, for the Justice Department's inspector general to lay out Steele's connections to Russian oligarchs—the information had been sitting at the FBI the whole time. Not until April 2020 did the public actually see evidence that even before Trump took office, the FBI had been receiving reports saying not only was the dossier garbage, but it was made up by some in the Russian government. That the subsources were interviewed by FBI agents and on record admitting it was "bar talk over beers."

Even though we eventually found out the truth, it was too late to undo the stain it had put on Trump's presidency. It was hard to undo the bad perception of a sitting president colluding against America, even though it was fiction. There were so many misleading and untruthful statements from sitting congressmen, who were Trump detractors, such as Representative Adam Schiff. He repeatedly went on television and said "there was collusion in plain sight" with no pushback at all from media, even though there was no evidence of this and during closed-door meetings in Congress, he said he did not have such evidence. This had a terrible impact on our country, dividing us, destroying the lives of people who were ensnarled in it, and creating an uncertain office of the presidency. Trump had a hard time recruiting some leading individuals to his administration because the story had left enough doubt in people's minds about Donald Trump's loyalty to America. This was an embarrassment for the greatest country in the world. Our country owes a great debt to those people who had the courage to step up, to tell the truth despite the attacks that certainly followed. Doug Collins is one of them. He is a truth teller. A man of conviction and courage and I have witnessed this firsthand. He worked tirelessly throughout his time in Washington to try and seek out truth. He questioned witnesses over when they first learned the people behind the dossier admitted they made it up. He demanded documents to be public, witness testimony to be reported. This is no small matter. Our constitution protects our freedom and liberty. But if and when bad actors weaponize the intelligence agencies of the US government, those freedoms can be compromised, if not lost.

Collins came on both my *Sunday Morning Futures* program on Fox News and my weekday program, *Mornings with Maria*, on Fox Business dozens of times over a four-year period, to combat the misinformation that my viewers were being assaulted by elsewhere. He takes you inside this extraordinary moment in time. It must be told over and over again. If the powers that be can make up a story of collusion about a sitting president, imagine what they could do to you or me, if it helps their cause. How would you like to be wrongly wiretapped for a year the way Trump aide Carter Page was? No charges were ever brought against Page despite this massive government overreach. This is against all we stand for. The need for honest brokers in Washington is critical to our democracy. We need representation of integrity and honesty. We need to know our representatives will work for the American people's interest. To follow every story no matter where it goes in the name of truth. Doug Collins did that. He is a patriot. He has earned my trust. And he is a truth teller.

Maria Bartiromo is the anchor of Fox News' Sunday Morning Futures *and* Mornings with Maria *on Fox Business. She is the co-author of* The Cost: Trump, China and American Revival.

INTRODUCTION

It was destined to happen, like the first time you saw the love of your life and thought to yourself, *One day, I will make them mine.* Destiny is a funny thing. It can take on a life of its own, and it flows and turns like a stream of water that has flowed outside its banks and begins to carve new paths in the land around it. These kinds of destiny are part of the natural order: love, new beginnings, and the trophy at the end of the pursuit of something that you have poured your whole life into. It's the destiny that we dream of that makes us get up and go, plan, and hope for more, believing that one day it will happen.

But there is also a dark side of destiny. It lines up with the worst intentions of man. It is the destiny that fulfills itself in a manic, myopic focus, with actions that become so intense that nothing else matters. This kind of focus causes you to believe that, in the end, if you cannot have the dream or the destiny that you want, you can create it, using any means and opportunities available. Unfortunately, this approach to destiny is the one that consumed the Democratic Party during Donald J. Trump's presidency.

Historians will look back at the events of the fall of 2019 and the impeachment of then-President Donald J. Trump, and they will debate the merits of the charges and the circumstances that surrounded the whole debacle. I will describe to you, in the pages to come, how the impeachment was not really about a phone call with a foreign leader, a supposed "quid pro quo," or how the president conducted himself. It was not even about a Russia investigation that had fizzled just months before the proceedings. No, I believe that what happened in the halls of Congress during this time was merely a date with a destiny dreamed of by Democrats still feeling the sting of bitter tears on the night that Donald Trump derailed the coronation of Hillary Clinton. It was on that night, when the mainstream media was stunned and brought to tears and the Washington establishment was shaken to its very core, that the seed was planted. *We may not have won tonight, but we will never let this stand*, they thought to themselves. Instead of plotting how to reconnect with the American people and try again in four years, the movement that could not believe what had happened began to look for another way—to plot a different course. Seeds had already been planted. The "other way" was the impeachment of the man who had stolen their dream. That—not acceptance, humility, or self-reflection—was the destiny sought by Washington Democrats following President Trump's election.

I do not believe that what happened in the fall of 2019 was solely the result of the phone call on July 25, 2019, between President Trump and Ukrainian President Volodymyr Zelensky. No matter what one thinks of that call, it was certainly not what caused the Democrats to file articles of impeachment. It was simply a tool placed in their hands, a means to an end. As the ranking member of the House Judiciary Committee, I was a witness to the proceedings that led to the impeachment of Donald Trump. My vantage point offered a unique view into the Democrats' one-track mind—not just on the Judiciary Committee but across their entire caucus when it came to dealing with President Trump. It was not that they did not like his policies or his agenda—differences envisioned and desired by our Founders. It was evident early on that they simply did not like him.

I would have liked to think that the reaction to the president was simply one born from policy disagreements. However, before the president was sworn in, there was already discussion of impeachment for everything from his business dealings to his personal attitudes and actions. The sad truth of this whole affair was that, in the end, the Democrats could not reconcile their disbelief that the American people had elected Donald Trump. In the end, in the minds of the Democrats, he had to be removed.

The story that played out in the fall of 2019 was a sham perpetrated not on Donald Trump but on the American people. Impeachment should never be a threat or a tool to carry out the wishes of a temporary congressional majority against a president they simply do not like. However, when power is your goal, and you are given the means and opportunity to extract a pound of flesh, then too many people will put aside rational thoughts to accomplish a political goal, under the guise of acting in the best interest of the American people.

Over the last twenty-five years, American politics have devolved into an ever-increasing polarization of one party against the other. The "benefits" of this polarization have largely been political victories, typically at the expense of the "other side." Since the impeachment of Bill Clinton in 1998, the use or threat of impeachment has been hurled at every president. The checks and balances envisioned by our Founders, including impeachment, have been weaponized to achieve specific political outcomes. President George W. Bush was threatened with impeachment over the wars in Iraq and Afghanistan. President Obama was threatened with impeachment over his healthcare plan known as "Obamacare." It is often said that once a threshold is crossed, it becomes easier to cross that threshold again and again.

In the fall of 2019, this polarization in search of political gain played out in a very public arena. It is the events leading up to that fateful fall that I will explore in this book. I believe that what happened during that impeachment process exemplified what we, as Americans, must not tolerate on the political stage. If we are to truly have a system of checks and balances, as envisioned by our Founding Fathers, then we must use the impeachment process as they intended: as a tool to remove those who have violated the public trust and damaged the American system of governance. It should never be used by any political party to further a political agenda or to avenge a perceived wrong.

In this case, after Democrats had engineered two and a half years of investigations and allegations, and the belief that the wrong candidate had been elected in 2016, they decided the time-honored American elections process, as designed by our Founders, would not achieve their political objectives. They were profoundly frustrated. They had promised the American people that investigations would prove Donald Trump was a corrupt candidate and, later, a corrupt president. It did not happen.

They had failed. But the embarrassment would not stand.

On July 24, 2019, Special Counsel Robert Mueller testified before the House Judiciary and Intelligence Committees. As Judiciary Committee ranking member, I led the questioning of Special Counsel Mueller on behalf of House Republicans. This hearing was the final chapter in closing out Special Counsel Mueller's investigation into the alleged Russian collusion with the Trump campaign. This was the moment Democrats had waited three long years for—the fulfillment of their destiny: the beginning of the end for President Trump.

Instead, what that hearing showed was that what Democrats had promised, the proof of a corrupt process and president, was not to be found—despite the expenditure of tens of millions of taxpayer dollars by the special counsel. It was at that moment that Democrats, who had been on a mission to prove President Trump was a corrupt leader, were left with little but empty threats and idle slanders. Simply put, Mueller did not deliver the goods.

However, Democrats were not done. On July 25, 2019, when most of the world was reading the results of Special Counsel Mueller's testimony before Congress, an alleged "whistleblower" decided the president had abused his power by allegedly threatening a foreign leader for his own personal and political benefit. That call would be the fuel that revived the promise made by Democrats to take down President Trump. The only problems became the "clock and the calendar." How Washington Democrats pulled off the impeachment of Donald Trump is a story of *rage* that an election had been lost, which led to an investigation that cost taxpayers millions of dollars and did not prove anything, and *retribution* against a man who had disrupted the system, had the audacity to run for and be elected president against the wishes of Washington Democrats, and had failed to give in to those who wanted to stop his administration from achieving success on behalf of the American people.

The table was set, and now was the time to finally impeach Donald Trump once and for all. The only problem that stood before the Democrats was whether they could do what it took to start and complete an impeachment before the 2020 election. The answer was, "Yes, we will," and I was on the front lines.

The clock was ticking, and the calendar was short. The rest is history.

* * * * *

To understand those seventy-eight days in the fall of 2019—to understand the passions and myopic focus of the Democrats—you first must remember the cause of their distress: the fact that Donald Trump had won the presidency in 2016. The shocking results of that election night left the Democratic Party in a state of shock and panic. Donald Trump was everything they did not want. He was loud, boisterous, and as far from politically correct as you could be. Yet somehow, he still upset the return of the Clinton machine to Washington, DC.

The Democrats, led by then-Minority Leader Nancy Pelosi and lame-duck, second-term President Barack Obama, had longed to return to the days of total Democrat control of the levers of power. Just a few short years earlier, Democrats controlled both the House and the Senate, and President Obama sat in the White House. In their rush to exploit their power, they embarked on an ambitious agenda that included a crippling of our health-care system and an overhaul of the financial system that led to chaos in our banks, especially those serving the rural and underserved parts of our population. It was a mandate they believed they had from the people and, in the words of President Obama's chief of staff, Rahm Emanuel, they could not "let a crisis go to waste."

However, by the time the 2016 presidential election cycle rolled around, the Democrats were facing a crisis. The Senate had flipped in the 2014 election cycle, giving Republicans control of Capitol Hill for the first time since 2006. The Democrats had little realistic hope of gaining control of the House or the Senate in the 2016 election cycle, so their focus centered on keeping the White House. If the Democrats could keep the White House, they thought, they could continue to impose progressive policies on the American people via executive fiat, check Republican efforts to cut taxes and spur freedom and economic growth, and hold out hope that they could eventually regain control of either the House or the Senate.

Innumerable books, documentaries, and articles have been written discussing the 2016 election. Republicans, seeing our shot at regaining control of the White House, attracted a field of over twenty candidates.

Most had no chance of winning, but the intoxicating power that comes with looking into a mirror and believing you could be president—and having willing consultants telling you that you have what it takes—was too much for many leaders to ignore.

The Republican field ranged from former Governors Mike Huckabee and Jeb Bush to Chris Christie and Scott Walker. Numerous United States senators—including Ted Cruz, Marco Rubio, and Rand Paul—took their places in the pantheon of conservative stars hoping to lead Republicans back to the White House. However, along came an outsider, one known not for a political career but for hosting a reality TV series and building skyscrapers that changed the face of New York City's skyline. On June 16, 2015, Donald Trump descended the escalator at Trump Tower and announced that he was running for president of the United States. On that day, most did not wonder whether he would be president, but why he would put himself out there amid this group of seasoned politicians who had all been planning and building up to this moment for years and years. The media and the political world looked on with a casual interest. For many, Donald Trump served as a fun distraction for what would be a long political grind.

Donald Trump was brash, boisterous, and carried an acerbic tongue. His rise brought to American politics a sharp edge that had not been seen in years, if ever before. He said what he felt and went after anyone who dared to attack him or his candidacy. As the campaign on the Republican side wore on, the field thinned, and to the horror of many in the mainstream media—and even the Republican Party—the one left standing was none other than the one who had not even been given a chance: Donald John Trump.

As the almost circus-like atmosphere played out on the Republican side, the Democrats were planning a continuation of the progressive policies of President Obama. The Democratic nominee for president would be Hillary Clinton. The question was never really in doubt. The stage was set for Hillary to become the first female president, and in the minds of the Democrats, no one would stop that from happening. It was her—and their—destiny.

One problem with that scenario, however, was someone forgot to tell Bernie Sanders. The democratic socialist from Vermont entered the race, even with the rules and the odds stacked against him. But in the end, the Clinton machine was too powerful, and the Democratic Party showed it was more concerned about controlling the narrative and the results than letting an outsider like Bernie, who energized the party's progressive base in ways that had not been seen in almost fifty years, ruin the party that had been set up for Hillary Clinton. As the slogan said, they were with *her.*

Politics has never been a gentle exchange of ideas while the public watches and makes an informed choice on who they want to represent them. The history of political campaigns has been filled with parades, speeches, posters, signs, buttons, and a healthy dose of every conceivable trick in the book to give one candidate the advantage over another. The public will tell pollsters and the occasional intrepid reporter when asked the question, "Do you like negative ads?" that they are turned off by them and do not like them at all. However, the not-so-subtle secret that all the pollsters know and the consultants who advise candidates on how to win a race will tell you is that it is just not true.

Growing up in the South—and especially in North Georgia—there are few things more sacred than church on Sunday, politics, NASCAR, and college football. These events are staples of conversation around the dinner table in restaurants and homes throughout the place that raised me. One day, I was discussing an upcoming NASCAR race, and I asked an older gentleman what he thought. He looked at me and said, "Watching the stock car racing is only good at the start and at the finish, the rest is just waiting to see how bad the wrecks are gonna be!"

That is probably a good description of auto racing, but it is an even better description of how Americans view political campaigns. We all claim to want the discussion of issues, but the main thing that moves the voter's choice is the wrecks that are produced by negative ads and the controversy that surrounds them. This cynical view of politics is normal to many, many people—whether or not it is politically correct. As a veteran of many political wars, I will say that a good contrast piece on your opponent is worth more than ten speeches given at the local Rotary Club or Republican Party meeting. Sure, you need to talk about what you want to do and convince people that you have a way to make their lives better. But at the end of the day, the only way that can happen is if you win. And the best path to that end is hardball: no holding back political heat. It would be nice if this were not the reality, but it is. And that is something for society to deal with and determine if this is what they want from their public officials.

The reason I bring it up in the context of the 2016 presidential race is not to highlight candidates on either side but to point to something that lays the groundwork for the seventy-eight days of impeachment in the fall of 2019. The normal political discourse took a turn toward a much darker place in this election. It started in the summer of 2016 when Donald Trump was the Republican Party nominee and Hillary Clinton was the Democrat nominee. The next part of this puzzle that led to the impeachment of Donald Trump was not the messaging of the campaigns, the constant barrage of insults, or the dark ads hurled in both directions during the campaign. The puzzle piece that pushed the country toward impeachment was playing out not on the campaign trail, but in the bowels of the federal government. Yes, you read that right. Members of the federal government were actively involving themselves in what appeared to be an attempt to influence a presidential election. This is not politics as usual; this is what has been feared by many Americans for years, and it was playing out behind the scenes with the thought that it would never be discovered because they thought there was no way that Donald Trump would be elected president. As we now know, they did not succeed in their plot. However, it would lead to one of the most expensive investigations in our country's history and, in its wake, tear down innocent people and poison the public's perception of its government and its role in our lives for years to come. The goal became to stop Donald Trump at all costs, and the world was about to be introduced to the names Robert Mueller, James Comey, Peter Strzok, Andrew McCabe, and Lisa Page. It was going to hear stories of salacious dossiers and conspiracies designed to weaken and eventually take down a president.

The story of the clock and the calendar that became the theme of the seventy-eight-day impeachment process in 2019 was activated in the spring of 2016. The boundaries were set, the adversaries were identified, and you could hear the smooth sound of sand falling through the hourglass. We were on a steady course for a political crisis.

PART ONE:

ALL THINGS RUSSIAN

CHAPTER 1:

THE INVESTIGATIONS: CLINTON TO MUELLER

Hillary Clinton has been at the center of American political dialogue for thirty years. She was a driving force behind her husband Bill Clinton while he was governor of Arkansas, and she was the glue that held together their surprising 1992 presidential campaign that successfully took out a sitting president, George H. W. Bush. It always appeared that whenever controversy broke out, Hillary was in the mix, providing a solution to pressing political problems such as the sexual affair scandal brought forth by Gennifer Flowers against Bill Clinton during his campaign for president. It was in that moment, when nothing but the equivalent of a bottom-of-the-ninth grand slam could save the candidacy, that Hillary stepped up. Seeing her sitting beside Bill on the couch during a *60 Minutes* interview assured the nation that, if she would stand by her husband, they could too.

After spending years helping Bill with his political career, she stepped forward when he left office and won a seat in the United States Senate. This office provided Hillary a way to remain in the national spotlight and build up her political credibility to run for president: the goal that she had set her sights on long before. Make no mistake, Hillary Clinton was no political novice and was not squeamish about the world of politics. She would never be content merely representing New Yorkers in the Senate. Hillary ran for the Democratic nomination for president in 2008 and lost. But she was rewarded by President Obama with a powerful seat in his cabinet as secretary of state, which burnished her résumé and raised her political profile even more. It was also from this high perch that the other aspects of the Clinton machine were elevated. Bill Clinton's foundation and its work benefited from Hillary's position, allowing Bill to stay intimately connected with foreign nations and leaders. However, during the middle of Hillary's tenure as secretary of state, an event that shook the world took place in Libya, in a town called Benghazi.

Little did we know at the time that the events surrounding that tragic night would have such far-reaching effects. It was through that tragedy, in which multiple American lives were lost, that investigations began on Capitol Hill that would have more of an impact on Hillary Clinton than her decisions surrounding Benghazi. It was discovered that Hillary Clinton did not believe she was subject to the same rules that others who served in the cabinet were bound by. She had designed and built a private email server that she would use during her tenure as secretary of state—a server that, as time and investigations revealed, contained classified information.

Now, much has been written and discussed about this email server and what was and was not on it. The fact that Hillary Clinton was not held responsible for her actions in handling classified information contributes to the perception that there are two systems of justice in this country: one for those who have influence, power, and money, and another for everyone else. This issue would persist into the 2016 presidential campaign, and that is where the story of the 2019 impeachment begins.

The investigation into Hillary Clinton's emails brought together at the Department of Justice a nucleus of investigators who, once the matter was dispensed with, would move to another investigation of a political figure—the investigation that became what the world now knows as Crossfire Hurricane, the investigation of alleged Russian interference in the 2016 presidential election.

THE SUMMER OF 2016

By June 2016, the political world was in turmoil. Democrats had succeeded in taking out Bernie Sanders and ensuring that Hillary Clinton would be their nominee. The dismantling of the Sanders campaign was the goal of the Democratic Party and the rules that they had set up. Congresswoman Debbie Wasserman Schultz was the head of the DNC and a Hillary supporter who made sure the nomination process would favor Hillary, who Democrats intended would be the first female president of the United States. However, one thing Democrats did not account for was that the American people, on both sides of the political spectrum, were more and more turned off by what they saw as politics as usual. The reasons for that depended on your political persuasion. If you were liberal and believed the government was not doing enough to solve the woes facing our country, a leader like Bernie Sanders appealed to you more than a career Democrat who said the right things but never furthered an agenda of radical change. This left the Democrats with a nominee who was, to their voter base, flawed at best. At worst, the Democrat base believed the election had been stolen from their preferred candidate, Senator Sanders.

Republicans were facing a different issue. In June 2016, it was apparent that Donald J. Trump would be the Republican nominee for president. This outsider, who had no tolerance for business as usual or politics that played by the same old script, had run over a field of twenty-plus candidates on his way to the nomination. He did this by being the kind of candidate people had, quietly, always wanted to see. He would say what he thought and would not back down if challenged or if someone was offended by what he said. He was an extraordinarily successful businessperson, unencumbered by any pressure to be something he was not to win votes or gain donors. He would simply go straight to the people, tell them America was the great hope of the world, and that the only thing keeping it from being great again was the politicians who, for decades, on both sides of the aisle, kept looking for the world's approbation or putting their own interests ahead of our country's.

I am from a very conservative area of Georgia, and no matter where I went, and no matter what setting, the one refrain I would hear over and over was, "Finally, someone is saying what I have been thinking!" Donald Trump issued a call for the country to turn out and fight for itself and to let the rest of the world know that the time of American leaders apologizing for our way of life was over. If you elected Donald Trump, he would "Make America Great Again." As 2016 wore on, the MAGA movement steadily gained steam. This was not lost on the Democratic candidate for president.

By mid-2016, the presidential campaign was into the home stretch, but Hillary Clinton still had a problem. The existence of her private email server was still dogging her campaign. And this was true even when FBI Director Comey went to amazing lengths—in my view, highly improperly—to announce the closure of the FBI investigation into Hillary's wrongdoing. The extraordinary press conference was summed up in an article in the *National Review* by David French on July 5, 2016, when he wrote:

> Rarely have 30 minutes of television so perfectly encapsulated the decline and fall of the rule of law and the extraordinary privileges enjoyed by America's liberal elite. After listing abuse after abuse—lie after lie—Comey declared that "no reasonable prosecutor" would prosecute Hillary for her obvious and manifest crimes. It is good to be a Clinton.

For most people, this was the first they saw of someone who became a central figure in the impeachment of Donald Trump. James Comey was the director of the FBI, having been appointed by President Obama in September 2013. Before assuming that position, he had served in multiple senior government roles, including as US attorney for the Southern District of New York in 2002 and 2003 and the deputy attorney general from December 2003 to August 2005. He served as the deputy to both John Ashcroft and Alberto Gonzales. He left to go into private legal practice but reentered public life as the FBI director in 2013.

Comey was described by associates who worked with him in his earlier stints at the Department of Justice as being very self-centered and career focused. He was competent, but his attitude and self-importance, as one former coworker put it, would enter the room ahead of him. It was this desire to be front and center that eventually led Comey to the stage that July day to deliver his meandering and frustrating attempt to exonerate Hillary Clinton. However, instead of squelching the storm around Hillary, Comey's press conference became more fuel for the fire that was already raging. It showed millions of Americans that the FBI would not hold Hillary Clinton to the same standards as everyone else. In another election year, she might have been able to maneuver out of this crisis, but this was no regular election. The American people were tired of politics as usual. They had never trusted Hillary, who had worn out her welcome on the national stage. They would not reward Hillary for her shady dealings by helping her realize her elusive dream of being the first female president of the United States of America.

While the Republican world was descending upon Cleveland, Ohio, in July 2016 for the Republican National Convention, the seeds of rabidly political, anti-Trump corruption were quietly growing among a group of rebels inside the Department of Justice. The group led by Peter Strzok, Lisa Page, and others was already worried about the possibility of Donald Trump becoming president. Their work behind the scenes with the use of a fraudulent dossier involving a man named Christopher Steele that was designed to take out Donald Trump would become the basis for what we will discuss in depth, and that is the Mueller investigation. Much has been written about this sordid time in the Department of Justice. The willful partisan action by these individuals scars the department to this day. Their actions set the table for what would end up in the fall of 2019 as the impeachment of Donald Trump. They may not have been able to stop him from becoming president, but they would do all they could to make his presidency difficult. I honestly believe that it was their work on what would become known as Operation Crossfire Hurricane that led to the sham impeachment.

ELECTION DAY 2018

In life, many times you think you understand the moment. The time you look into the eyes of that person you love and you commit yourself to them for the rest of your life, or when you welcome a child into the world, or when you say goodbye to a loved one who has passed from this life and into eternity. The reality is that what you understand in the moment is what you see and feel or the preconceived notions of what the events entail. It is impossible to know where your marriage will take you, how your children will lead you on an emotional roller coaster of love that never stops, and what loneliness or regret may come in the days and weeks after the death of that special person. Things we do not control in the moment provide the unexpected adventures in life and the events that come along with them.

The election on November 6, 2018, was one of those events that did not just bring winners and losers to offices across the country. It provided the opportunity that Nancy Pelosi, Jerrold Nadler, Adam Schiff, and other Democrats had been seeking for two years.

Ever since that fateful night when Donald Trump shocked the world, these Washington Democrats had been looking for the opportunity to do what they felt the American people should have done, and that is to keep this man, who spoke of putting America first, out of the White House. Make no mistake, the Democrats were intent on fixing what they perceived as a "mistake" by the American people. They had been trying for two years to convince the world that Donald Trump was not fit to serve as president of the United States. They ranted, they yelled, and they pitched petulant fits on the floor of the House of Representatives. The Democrats and their accomplices in the media held up people such as James Comey and Robert Mueller, individuals they may, in the past, have viewed as Republicans and opponents, as heroes standing up to the corrupt man in the White House. They fought to keep the Mueller investigation going and, along the way, had even gotten some Republican elected officials to go along with them. But at the end of the day, for all their resistance, their efforts called to mind the line from Macbeth that discusses the brevity of life. They strutted and fretted their hour upon the stage, telling their tale full of sound and fury, signifying nothing.

That is, until Election Day 2018 gave them new life.

The Democrats had taken back the United States House, and Nancy Pelosi was on her way to becoming Speaker again. What we did not fully know that night was the extent the Democrats would go to enact their vengeance on President Trump—and, by extension, on the people who elected him. The reckoning would not stop until Democrats had removed the stain of Donald Trump's presidency from the national stage.

Leading up to the election in 2018, I traveled all over the country as the vice-chairman of the House Republican Conference, to maintain our House majority. The odds were not in our favor, since historically, the party in power loses seats in the first midterm election after a new president has been elected.

And we were the party in power. We controlled the House, the Senate, and the presidency. During that time, we had passed historic tax reform, cut back on burdensome regulations, and restored money to our depleted military, and the president had embarked on an ambitious trade agenda that would make our trade deals more favorable for all parties. The economy was growing, and so was the stock market. America was prospering.

However, the relentless attacks by the Democrats and their mainstream media allies had penetrated in many parts of suburban America. The attacks on immigration, especially the issue of illegal immigrant families and unaccompanied minors, which Democrats conveniently forgot was started under President Obama, were effective. The truth would not ruin Democrats' political narrative. The press would ensure they did not either.

The other issue that sat front and center in the lead-up to the election was health care. The new president and congressional leadership decided to tackle health care first in the 115th Congress. The battle against Obamacare was a long-running battle—but a worthy one. Now that we controlled both houses of Congress and the White House, it was time to attack this bad law that had made health care worse in this country, especially in rural districts like mine. Health-care choices and prices had skyrocketed over the past eight years, and we had promised our voters we would address that.

But it was not that simple. After almost nine months, our efforts failed when the late Senator John McCain chose to vote "no" on a Senate "skinny repeal" bill. That bill, while far from ideal, would have at least resulted in a conference committee between the House and the Senate to finalize a bill that would work. Instead of moving the ball forward, Senator McCain voted to kill the effort to repeal and replace Obamacare. With that, Democrats had their wedge issue for the election.

As I traveled that fall from California to Minnesota, to Nebraska and Florida, and, of course, across my home state of Georgia, we were feeling the winds of resistance. During a trip to Minnesota to support our candidate and future congressman Pete Stauber, I remember talking with Republicans who were genuinely concerned about the failure of our efforts to overturn Obamacare. It had been a promise without qualification made to our voters since the day it was passed, and they could not understand why, with control of all three parts of the legislative process, we could not get it accomplished.

On the other side, the Democrats were taking advantage of the failure by falsely claiming Republicans would have denied care to those with preexisting conditions. These attacks were false, but to people who were already hurting under the health-care law, they were effective. And many of our members and candidates did not do a good job responding to those attacks.

President Trump worked hard on the campaign trail, and in the end, we retained control of the Senate, even picking up two seats. However, Democrats picked up forty-one seats and took control of the House of Representatives.

The election results meant that the power structure of the House would shift from Republican control to Democratic control. The new Speaker would be Nancy Pelosi, and Steny Hoyer would be the new majority leader. They would lead the Democrats in taking over all the positions of power in the House, including committee chairmanships. They would now not only have the opportunity to harass President Trump and obstruct his agenda, but they would have the full resources of the House of Representatives to carry out their plans.

THE CHANGE BEGINS

Americans are familiar with the elections process in our country, and most understand that elections have consequences. The party that wins reaps the benefit, and the other side regroups and goes from leading to defending. This is a big change in mindset for members of Congress—many of whom had never served in the minority of a legislative body. The reality is that in the minority, especially in the House, you may accomplish very few, if any, of the goals you have set for your time in office. Unlike the Senate, the House is a majoritarian institution. The framers designed it that way. The party in the majority controls all the levers of power. That means that bills you were working on might be banished to the ash heap of history—or, worse, if your idea was good and had bipartisan appeal, your bill might be reintroduced by a member of the majority, who would then be able to claim the idea as their own.

Much of the legislative work in the House is done by the various committees. Generally, all members, other than the leadership, serve on at least one legislative committee. The party that controls the House controls the committees and their agendas. A change in party control, therefore, means that the committees you served on, and in which your party got to control the agenda, will now be controlled by those that you have fought against in the previous Congress.

All this, despite the seemingly harsh nature of it, is normal and part of our country's history. There is a reason for the old saying, "There are two things you don't want to see made—sausages and laws." The framers, in their wisdom, designed our national legislature to be oppositional in nature. It serves as a reminder to each member of Congress that it is not just your job to score political points in Washington, DC, against the other side. If those points do not have voter support or favor, you will wind up as the minority on the outside looking in instead of controlling the legislative agenda.

In the weeks after an election in which party control shifts, the process of change is put into place. The first thing that happens is that each side gathers with their membership, both returning members and those that were newly elected, to elect the leadership teams for each party. In the case of the Democrats, it meant deciding whether Nancy Pelosi would again become Speaker of the House. With forty-one new members, many of whom were much more liberal than the previous makeup of the Democratic Caucus, the path was not as easy as one may think for the person who served as the first female House Speaker and had led Democrats back into the majority. The one thing that can be said in Washington, DC, however, is that Nancy Pelosi is a very savvy political operator who has maintained a firm grip on her leadership post by knowing how to appeal to her members' needs and who possesses the ability to balance reward and punishment to keep the membership in line. After securing the requisite number of votes, which included allowing some far-left members who needed to vote against her to do so, Nancy Pelosi was once again elected Speaker and thus controlled the levers of power once again in the House. She would decide the committee chairmen and the makeup of committees going into the 116th Congress. It would be those decisions that would put in motion the impeachment of Donald Trump. Democrats had campaigned on the impeachment of the president. It was not a matter of if. It was a matter of when.

On the Republican side, we had choices to make as well. After what was a crushing defeat in the November election, we had to prepare ourselves for life in the minority. Kevin McCarthy, who had served as majority leader in the 115th Congress, hoped we would hold the majority, and he would have the opportunity to become Speaker with the retirement of Paul Ryan. This was the moment that the likable member from California had been waiting for. However, instead of being Speaker, he would have to transition being the leader of the minority. Representative Steve Scalise from Louisiana would transition from majority whip (the number three leadership position in the majority) to the minority whip (the number two leadership position in the minority).

As Republicans met to elect our leaders, you could feel a palpable difference in our conference. Many were still in shock; they could not believe we had lost forty-one seats and been relegated to the minority. As we gathered after the election, the one thing that surprised me was that many of our members acted as if nothing had changed, as if they would still get to pass bills and decide what they wanted to do on the committees they served on. One morning, when we gathered for our weekly conference meeting, Representative Tom Cole from Oklahoma, who was regarded in the conference as a wise and competent leader, was speaking to a member who came up to him about a piece of legislation the member wanted to introduce in the next Congress. I overheard Congressman Cole say that the member needed to understand: the idea was good, but the reality was that the bill would not get passed. When the member pushed back and tried to say, "Well, how could it be done?" the wise veteran Cole simply looked at him and said, "That's nice. But you must remember that you are in the minority now. Victories will only come again when we are in the majority."

The member looked at him for a moment as if he did not understand the words coming out of Cole's mouth and then slowly walked away with his head down. The sting of defeat for the conference was becoming real. No longer could we have discussions and fights in Room 215 of the Capitol about what we would do or how we would do it. Instead, we would be relegated to a small room in the Capitol Visitor Center to plot and plan how to react in the new world of a Pelosi speakership and what would become a relentless attack on the president and one of the most progressive agendas ever to be rolled out.

With the Senate still in Republican control, none of the Democrats radical ideas would become law, but it was not about making law for the Democrats at this time. It was about placing a marker for those liberal causes that had supported them and, at the same time, laying a foundation to make sure that Donald Trump would not win reelection. To combat what lay ahead, the Republicans in the House would have to change their mindset and change quickly. The best offense would have to be the best defense. The whole focus would need to become slowing the Democrat agenda and making the case that the voters had made a mistake in letting the Democrats claim the majority so that we could regain legislative control in two years. Little did we know that the Democratic agenda would become not one of achievable political results but a manic obsession over Donald Trump.

The battlefield for the upcoming Congress was going to be in the committees of the House. The battles had been brewing for the last two years in the Intelligence Committee with Chairman Devin Nunes and Ranking Member Adam Schiff. These two would continue their battle in different chairs in the 116th Congress. The battle lines drawn and the bad blood present, the Intelligence Committee, which historically has been one of the most bipartisan committees, had become a battleground of opposing sides, in which the Democrat preoccupation with the president overflowed into all areas of the committee's work. Interestingly, however, in the new Congress, big changes were coming to two committees that would be front and center in the fallout from the Democratic push against the president. The House Oversight Committee had been chaired by the tenacious and particularly good prosecutor out of South Carolina, Trey Gowdy. Trey had decided, however, to retire and would not be returning to Congress. In the House Judiciary Committee, Bob Goodlatte from Virginia was also retiring. Chairman Goodlatte had led a very productive six years as the chairman of the committee, overseeing big pieces of legislation affecting criminal justice reform and copyright and intellectual property rights. These two members also led the joint investigation into the Department of Justice's investigations of Hillary Clinton and then-candidate Trump. That work led to the world becoming familiar with the exploits of James Comey, Peter Strzok, Lisa Page, Andrew McCabe, and Bruce and Nellie Ohr, just to name a few. Now with the new Congress coming in and the Republicans losing the chairmanships of these committees, the work for the minority would be to try and defeat the agenda of the new Democratic leadership in these committees.

The inner workings of Congress are, for the most part, foreign to most people in the country. The outwardly visible work, debating and making laws, is known, but the internal mechanics—or the "sausage making" process, as it has been referred to—is hidden from public view. I will tell you as an insider that no matter how transparent the art of legislating is, the decisions of internal party positions and politics are hidden from view and controlled by only a few. Think of it as voting on the class president in your high school but with major consequences for the future of the country hanging on these outcomes. How the different parties determine who serves on committees and who leads them are determined by the parties' leadership and the steering committee.

The Republican Caucus steering committee comprises members that are elected by their peers from regions of the country broken down by state delegations designed to have equal representation for each area of the country based on how many Republican members are from that part of the country. The fewer elected members, the larger the group of states put together to form a group that selects a member to represent the needs of that area on the steering committee. The main power in the steering committee is the leadership. The Republican leadership, the Speaker (when we are in the majority), the leader, and the whip all carry more than one vote. It is rare when the leadership doesn't get their way when it comes to decisions on the steering committee.

The steering committee makes decisions with a simple majority vote. It is a bit easier in the majority because the majority has control of setting the number that will be on each committee. In the minority, it is tougher because there are fewer slots and even the possibility of members losing their seats on certain committees.

The steering committee is a big deal, and members treat it like a campaign, complete with flyers and contact strategy to woo the members of the committee and especially leadership to see the reasons that you want a particular committee or position on that committee. The steering committee process has been criticized many times as being unfair and only benefiting those who play by the rules and do not cause leadership any headaches.

It is argued that it often does not prioritize experience or expertise by members but instead focuses on the intangibles of being a team player and the willingness to help the Republican Conference goals. This struggle for control of the steering committee led Paul Ryan to make changes to the voting structure of the committee when he agreed to become Speaker of the House. It was the push by the Freedom Caucus that precipitated the move that took some power from the leadership and gave it back to the rank-and-file membership. Make no mistake, however, the move was a step in a more democratic direction for decisions of the committee, but the power still resides with the leadership to shape and direct the placement of members.

In 2018, after the leadership elections were done, the work of the steering committee was upon us. I served on this committee for the previous Congress because of my position on the leadership team as the vice-chairman of the House Republican Conference. I knew going into this round of discussions before the committee would take on special meaning for me because I had set out to be the top Republican on the Judiciary Committee.

Looking back on the 2018 election cycle, I had worked extremely hard to keep the majority because if we did keep the majority, I was going to run for the chair of the Judiciary Committee. I would be just going into my fourth term, which in the history of Congress would have been one of the fastest rises to chairman of this committee. It was not a stretch for us to try. Despite what most think, there has been a great deal of turnover in the Congress in the past decade, and what used to take a long time by seniority was now cut down due to retirements, changes of committees, and people losing their seats or moving to other offices.

In my three terms, I had put my entire focus on the Judiciary Committee and honed my procedural skills by serving on the Rules Committee, in which we did battle with the Democrats on the bills that would be on the floor each week for debate. The one thing that I see too often in members of Congress is that they are not challenged or stretched in their thinking or their debate skills. I believe that most members are bored. They have bought the line that they are to fall into the pattern of raising money, making the right votes, and doing the right media and they will have a long tenure in the House of Representatives. I believe that is the very thing that is killing the body politic. Members should be challenging themselves and engaging in the debate that surrounds them. They need to be on the floor, present in committees and not just making a five-minute sound bite but looking for issues that they are passionate about and working to make the change that they want to see made in these areas.

I was told when I got to Congress by then-Majority Leader Eric Cantor of Virginia that the best thing for me to do was to find areas I was interested in and become an expert in those areas. Leader Cantor said that when people see you know what you are talking about in these areas, they will know that you are the person they can go to for help and advice on that subject. It was advice that I never forgot, and with the help of my staff, I set forth to become knowledgeable in all areas of the Judiciary Committee jurisdiction. I especially focused on those areas that affected many people and businesses but that were not as high profile as guns, abortion, and immigration, which the committee also handled.

The areas that I focused on and became expert in were the areas of copyright, patent and intellectual property, and criminal justice reform. It was this focus that allowed us to pass more pieces of major legislation in my short time in Congress than many members do in a decades-long career. It was all about focus and remembering that the people in my district did not elect me to simply exist in Congress. They wanted to see their member work to make their lives better.

This focus led us to pass bills such as the Cloud Act, which has come to define how data is stored and how our privacy is maintained while balancing the needs of law enforcement access when dealing with data stored all over the world. The Defending Trade Secrets Act works for the first time to stop the billions of dollars a year theft of trade secrets from our domestic companies, much of that knowledge being taken to China. This saves not only the technology but keeps jobs and innovation here in the United States.

Another bill, the Music Modernization Act, looked at the music industry and acknowledged that the change in the way our music is consumed, especially in the era of streaming, should be equitable for those not only who put out the music on their platforms but for all of those who have a part in the making of the music that touches our lives. I found that many of those who wrote the songs that become the soundtrack of our lives were shackled to an outdated legal arrangement that originated in some cases over one hundred years ago, which kept them from being able to get a fair price for their labor. The bill gave technology a way to not only provide our entertainment but also to keep the pipeline open so that we can continue to grow and expand the creative genius that is born in living rooms, garages, and anywhere music is written and performed. Those songwriters would be able to thrive, knowing that they could work hard and not only have their music heard but they could make a living at it as well. This bill took almost six years and many hours of work to get passed but in the end, lives are improved by the work that was accomplished.

We also passed several pieces of criminal justice legislation, such as the Comprehensive Criminal Justice and Mental Health Act, which provides our law enforcement with more training in how to deal with those with mental health conditions that they encounter while out patrolling.

It also led to the passage of the First Step Act. The First Step Act was the first major piece of criminal justice reform passed in decades. It has made the difference in many lives and given hope to many who have been trapped in our criminal justice system. President Trump and his son-in-law Jared Kushner were instrumental in the passage of this bill. The work by President Trump to take on an issue that has such a profound effect on many in our minority communities is one reason his support among African Americans rose during his presidency. For the first time, many who had only heard promises of what may come from Democratic administrations finally had real results from a president who said, "I care about you."

I am proud of these accomplishments and the fact that Washington can still be a place where things can get done and people's lives can be made better. It is also the reason that I wanted to be the chairman of the Judiciary Committee. Conservatives, I believe, have the best ideas because we believe in the individual and their power to thrive. We believe that by passing legislation that gets government out of people's lives and upholds the basic value of every individual, we are not only doing what is right, but we are also helping ensure that the future of our Republic is strong.

I believe that hard work still matters and that, with the right push, we could make the committee stronger and help the Trump administration build on its previous successes. In knowing how to fight and pass legislation, as well as working each week to hone my skills on the floor of the House sparring with the Democrats on the floor, I believed it was time to move up, and I knew I could convince the steering committee that I was the best one for the job.

The election of 2018 did not change my resolve to get things done, but I knew that my pitch would have to change. Instead of chairman, I would be the ranking member, the leader of the Republicans on the Judiciary Committee. In making the change, I drew upon my days on the Rules Committee and laid out a plan that I would share with the committee that said where we can find agreement to move good bills I will work hard to make that happen, but knowing that the Democrats would not be content to work with us I developed the battle plan that would carry the committee into the next phase: fight the Democratic Agenda to turn back our freedoms and progress with every rhetorical and procedural tactic available to us. I would make the Judiciary Committee the standard for how you fight in the minority.

The way the steering committee operates is that for each of the ranking member positions that are open, the committee schedules a time in which those who want to serve can make their case. You are asked to put together a presentation of about ten minutes in which you make your pitch as to why you should be chosen. Then, you are subjected to questions by the members. After all candidates have presented their case, the committee deliberates and then votes. Seems simple enough, but the reality is that if you want to win, you must have met with the committee members several times beforehand. And just as when you run for the office you hold, you have to have a winning campaign to navigate the politics of the committee. You may have a strong case, but if it is felt that there are too many in leadership from a certain part of the country or that you were not supportive of the agenda of a steering committee member, you would need to either solve the issue or get enough support to overcome the opposition.

I know many of you reading this are thinking: *Are you telling me that this is how it works?* In the end, it is a higher-stakes version of your high school class officer elections. Nobody ever said that Congress was complicated. In fact, if more would realize that the body is made up of many people just like them, we would begin to understand that those in office and those whom they serve are alike and that we need each other if we are to have a government that truly looks after the needs of the people.

The day arrived for our presentations to the steering committee. I arrived early and sat in the holding room waiting for the committee to be ready. In the days leading up to the meeting, I felt good about our run and felt we had the support of the members in the room. But still, questions lingered. I was a newer member compared to some. And while my media presence was good, I was not on the TV all the time, making the case about the issues we were dealing with. Even so, I had the trust of the members and was known as someone who would work hard and look after the issues that our conference was going to face in the next Congress. I knew that our committee would be the center of a lot of the Democrats' focus, and I had expressed that I was the best one to lead our conference in explaining our position to the American people and putting ourselves in the position of winning back the majority in the next election cycle.

Although it had been rumored that Representative Jim Jordan of Ohio would seek the position, he chose not to. That left only Representative Steve Chabot from Ohio to challenge me for the position of ranking member on the Judiciary Committee. Steve is a good member who was on his second tenure in the House. He had previously served in the House from 1995 to 2008, when he lost in the Obama presidential wave, and then was reelected to the House in 2010. He had a long history on the Judiciary Committee. He even served as an impeachment manager in the impeachment of President Bill Clinton. As the talk of investigations from the Democrats had grown louder since the election, I knew that his experience with impeachment would be an advantage, but in the end, the focus had to be broader, and that was the pitch that I made.

My years of not only public service but also ministry have afforded me opportunities to speak to many people in various settings, from small two- to three-person groups to thousands under tents and in auditoriums. All that experience, although good, never can prepare you to speak in front of what is, in essence, a jury of your peers. I came in that day with confidence but with a nervousness that I had not faced in years. My time had come, and it was now time to show why I should lead the Republicans on the committee. I laid out a two-fold path. On the one hand, I articulated that we needed to use the next two years leading up to the 2020 election cycle to fight for our agenda, working with the Democrats if they were willing but being prepared through a variety of techniques to fight back on their proposals with better ones of our own that we could explain to the American people. The other was that we had to prepare for being in the minority, and that meant that our job was to prepare for the investigations to come. I laid out a plan for a beefed-up communications team for the staff that would counter in real time the push by Jerrold Nadler and his committee, and we needed to beef up our investigation team for the committee staff to handle what would surely be a committee dominated by the theatrics of the majority in their attacks on the administration and President Trump. I explained that our emphasis must be on making the Democrats work for everything that they got. We may be the minority, but we had tools at our disposal. And we must be willing to put in the work to force them into following the rules or pay a price, both in the workings of the committee and in the media.

I made the comment to them, and I have repeated it many times since, that I believed as ranking member of the Judiciary Committee my job was to fight for the conservative values we believed in. My job was to make Chairman Nadler wake up every day, look at what he wanted to accomplish, and think, *What am I going to do about Collins and the rest of the Republicans on Judiciary?* If they wanted to bring in the storm of investigations and put on a show, I knew my job would be to make sure our side was ready to expose the show and beat them where we could.

The sentiment I expressed to the committee that day, and I believe the feeling already among the members of the steering committee, was that they may have the gavels, but our job was to not give them any easy breaths. After the steering committee deliberated, I received a call from Rep. Tom Graves, my colleague from Georgia with whom I had served both on the state level and in Congress. He called to congratulate me and tell me I was the new ranking member.

As a moment of celebration swept over me, I could not imagine what the next Congress would hold, but I knew that I was going to have a big part in it. Little did I know just how prophetic that thought would become. Now it was time to do the job. This state trooper's kid from North Georgia was about to step onto a big stage that would command the attention of the world for a time. The story that had been in the making since November 2016 was now about to unfold, and I would have a front seat. The clock and calendar were set, but as 2018 came to an end, little did we know how historic the next year would become.

After the excitement of the Steering Committee wore off, it was time to get to work on the process of putting together a committee staff as well as looking for new members to be a part of the committee. This was going to be difficult, especially with the staff, because instead of being in the majority, as we had been for eight years, we had to transition into the minority, which meant the size of our staff would be cut in half. I knew what we needed to prepare for, and I would have to have a team that could function not only in their area of expertise but also be willing to help with the investigations that we knew were coming. It is never easy to have to downsize staff. It is even more frustrating to know you must downsize while the opposition was going to upsize, and they were going to bring in outside help to focus them on going after President Trump.

One of the first meetings that I felt needed to happen was one with the incoming chairman of the Judiciary Committee, Jerrold Nadler. Jerry Nadler represents the Tenth Congressional District in New York. He has been in Congress since 1992, representing Manhattan. In fact, except by just a few blocks he would have been President Trump's congressman the way the lines are drawn in the city.

Jerry, as he is known, has had an ongoing confrontational relationship with President Trump going back to the 1980s when he was an assemblyman in the New York Legislature and then-developer Donald Trump was making plans for the Hudson Yards project. This was an exceptionally large project built on the site of a railroad terminal in the city. Nadler was opposed to the plan, and he was constantly fighting with Trump to stop the project and keep the rail yard. In the end, the compromise project was built, and Nadler, still opposed, said in his own words that he felt like he personally had lost because the project was built and the rail yard shut down. In listening to Chairman Nadler talk about those early dealings with Donald Trump, you can tell that he did not like him then, calling him unscrupulous and saying that Mr. Trump only got what he wanted by pushing others around and using his wealth. The early competition between the two would continue. Who would have guessed that the animosity that started so long ago would lead to another confrontation? However, this time, Jerry Nadler felt that he was in the driver's seat and President Trump would have to deal with him now. And in talking to the chairman over time, I could tell that made him happy.

We called to set up a meeting in which we would go over general issues of structure for the committee, such as staff office space and the number of staff we could keep for our side of the committee. I also wanted to use this time to feel out the chairman about his plans and thoughts for how he wanted to run the committee. I had hoped that he would want to continue some of the projects that we had worked on together in the past, such as criminal justice reform, intellectual property, and patent reform. I knew that we had plenty we would disagree on, but I still wanted to go in with an open mind to at least the first meeting to see what was on his mind.

The meeting took place in his office late one afternoon in December. I brought with me Brendan Belair, who was my chief of staff and would transition to being the staff director for our work on the committee. We were met by Chairman Nadler and three of his senior staff. He looked tired when I entered; he had had to endure a fight to get to sit as chairman. Just as I had encountered competition in my quest to become ranking member, Jerry had faced a strong challenge from Congresswoman Zoe Lofgren from California. In the end, Jerry had to use his experience as an impeachment manager in the Clinton impeachment to make the case as to why he should be the chairman. The world was put on notice that just being a liberal congressman from New York was not good enough. No, if he was going to lead the Judiciary Committee, he had to give in to the loud voices who disliked the president and commit to making the next Congress not about actual accomplishments but about finding a way to get President Trump.

Now I had worked with Jerry before in previous Congresses, and although we were ideologically opposed on practically everything, we were able to find common ground and get some ideas put into law. So, my hope was that we could take our new roles and find some solutions of common interest and that would leave time for fighting all the other things we disagreed upon. The thing I was not prepared for was that there was no interest in working together. In fact, the tone of the meeting was edgy, and I could tell that the agenda they had to push was all about President Trump—and that investigating him would be the main thing on their mind. This became very apparent to me when I brought up criminal justice reform. We had just finished up the First Step Act, which President Trump had signed into law, and we all knew that for all the good the bill did, it was crucial that we follow up with oversight from the committee to ensure that the bill was implemented properly. I was stunned that when I brought this up, he looked at me and dismissed it with a quick "Yeah, that is fine, but we have a lot of things we need to do first." The tone of the meeting never got better. What I had hoped would be a meeting to find common ground became a discussion of what they would do, and it all pointed back at the president. I could not even get him to commit to anything that could have been productive and possibly bipartisan. The seething dislike for the president permeated the meeting and manifested in what would become the theme of the new Congress. That theme was we have our agenda, and we will not let anything get in our way.

The rancor that was felt in that meeting was also carried out in very petty ways during the transition leading up to the new Congress. The previous chairman, Bob Goodlatte, had been very accommodating to the minority. He would let them go on and on in hearings and markups without moving to shut them down. The only time he did move to shut them down was after almost ten hours of debate on the rules of the committee that had turned into nothing but one long infomercial of the Democratic Party's problems with the President Donald Trump. Chairman Goodlatte had also allowed some minority staff to have offices in the basement of the Rayburn House office building so they could be closer to the committee room and for convenience for the members of the committee to access. At first, the new Democratic majority wanted to cut our staff almost completely out of the House office building and across the Street to the Ford House office building.

The pettiness set the tone for what would become a momentous year ahead. After many discussions, in which we pointed out the pettiness of their actions and the fact that they had been treated far better than they were treating us, they somewhat relented and gave us an old committee room in which we had to put staff in makeshift offices. The Democrats were making one thing clear: the new majority would not let anything get in their way. They did not care what the perception was or whom they ran over. They were going to go all out to push a very leftist agenda, and they were going to find a way to get President Trump. It was a little bit after this meeting that we found out through the reporting of an overheard phone conversation of Chairman Nadler that the first thing they wanted to do was to have a hearing featuring Acting Attorney General Matt Whitaker. The game was on. The story line was set. All that was needed now was the new Congress to come into session, and the clock and calendar would be put into motion. They had Mueller in the wings, and they wanted to lay the groundwork for what they thought would be the fatal blow to the president, the report by Robert Mueller. Nothing else mattered. It was all about one person, who just happened to be the president of the United States.

However, I believe that Jerry Nadler, in his dislike and rush to get the president, forgot something that he shared with me during a committee meeting the following year. I asked him about his past with the president, and he talked about the many run-ins that they had had over the years. He talked about the various projects and how he did not like the president's style. Then, for some reason, I asked him if he ever won any of those battles. He looked at me, then looked away and said, "No." It was in that admission that I could see the flame burned bright in Jerry Nadler to not lose this time.

January 2019 arrived with a burst of excitement in Washington, DC. The press was giddy with excitement, it seemed, at the prospect of

Nancy Pelosi taking back over as Speaker. I am a Republican who has found it rather a waste of time to complain about the media, especially about the disparate treatment it gives in covering the inner workings of the Democratic Conference and the Republican Conference. Now I know that many folks, especially conservatives, would not agree with me that this is a waste of time, but let me explain. When conservatives are constantly complaining about the media and the help that they seemingly give to the Democrats, we are wasting time that we could be using to find new ways to get our message out. I am a firm believer that most people understand the bias; they do not need to keep hearing it. They want to know what they can do to fight it and if we are going to use every means we can to move ahead anyway. Media bias against conservatives is a fact that we live with. Winners do not waste time with things they don't control; they go out and change the narrative. With the new Democratic majority coming in, the bias would be on full display. In January 2019, Nancy Pelosi still had one more step to make before she could officially take over the speakership, a floor vote of the whole membership of the House. She went on to gain 220 votes and secured the speakership; however, she lost fifteen Democrats in the process. This in and of itself is not really a story to most people in America. Speaker Pelosi worked her conference and secured the votes she needed, as any leader would do. The reason that I bring it up is to give you a reference point to what we would face from the media during the 116th Congress especially during the run-up to impeachment and beyond.

The fact that Speaker Pelosi lost some votes in her conference was not unexpected, but to those of us on the Republican side, it showed the true leanings in the media by the way the story was portrayed. CNN reported that although Pelosi had some opposition, she worked her caucus and secured the votes needed to govern. There were no headlines about the vast divide in the Democratic Conference. No breathless discussion of what it meant that so many had voted against her. No, just the acceptance and triumph that Speaker Pelosi had done it again and shown she was the master at counting the votes in her conference.

The sad part about these same reporters is that during the previous two Speakers' elections they all were writing daily stories about the votes that Speaker John Boehner had lost and the ones that were not satisfied with Speaker Paul Ryan who followed Boehner. The stories were not about how masterful John Boehner was at getting the votes he needed to be Speaker. Instead, the stories talked of the dissension in the ranks of the Republican majority and the questioning of whether we could really get anything done. Again, most Americans simply want to know what is going on in Washington, DC, and can make up their own minds as to the issues. But as we would see throughout the entire 116th Congress, the story would never be as the old saying goes, "Just the facts, please." It would be a constant battle to overcome the Democrats and the media, who had one common enemy: President Donald Trump. For anyone who harbored thoughts that the new Democratic majority would focus on governing, those thoughts were put to rest rather quickly when Rashida Tlaib, a new congresswoman from Michigan, gave a summation of why she was in Washington. Speaking at an event for supporters shortly after she was sworn in, Tlaib, the first Palestinian American elected to Congress, recalled a conversation she had had after she won: "And when your son looks at you and says, 'Mama, look, you won. Bullies don't win,' and I said, 'Baby, they don't'—because we're going to go in there and we're going to impeach the motherf*****r."

There was not a lot of searching for common ground with this group of newly elected legislators.

Back in the Judiciary Committee, fueled by the anger expressed by Congresswoman Tlaib, the stage was set, and the first show was about to begin. Chairman Jerry Nadler was hell-bent on calling Acting Attorney General Matt Whitaker to testify before the committee even though William Barr was already awaiting confirmation in the Senate to assume the job. The reason for this hearing was not about the facts or even what Whitaker could bring to the table. It was about laying the groundwork to make the case to the American people that the Trump administration was corrupt and that the officials the president appointed were not public servants but lackeys for the administration. However, before those hearings, I knew that I needed to have some time with my new committee to get everyone on the same page. It was going to be a fight, but we had to fight smart. The goal was to make the Democrats answer for the plan they were executing, not for us to be the story.

Going into the 116th Congress, the Judiciary Committee, especially on the Republican side, had undergone a lot of changes. Many members who were on the committee had, over time, moved on or retired. In fact, the two members who had led the investigations into Operation Crossfire Hurricane, Chairman Bob Goodlatte and Chairman Trey Gowdy, had both retired. That meant that going into the 116th Congress, the Republican side would be starting with a mix of old faces, and some new ones as well.

I was taking on the leadership of a group that was frustrated by the loss of the election but even more incensed that the Democrats were going to spend all their time going down the path of investigation and harassment of the president. We understood elections had consequences, but we were even more resolved to stand for our values and the rights of the minority in the House even if the Democrats wanted to walk all over those very rights that had most recently given them a voice during their time in the minority. The first thing that I wanted to do was to prepare our side for the new state of battle we were about to enter, so after getting our new members assigned, we had a day of preparation with the committee members.

One of the great things that happens every election cycle in Washington is that change is constant. You are constantly seeing members move on and new members take their place. The not-so-hidden secret on the Hill is that it is not the members who provide the long-term continuity on the committees but the staff who work on those committees. The staff on committees are the ones who are the subject matter experts on the work and issues before the committee. Many have been with the same committee for an awfully long time and truly are the most valuable resources that committee members can call on for help while serving on the committee. The first thing that I had had to do was hire the staff who was going to stay and bring on new staff to help in our new role of investigators. This is a unique aspect to Washington. Although many committee staffers have had their jobs for many years, they are still on what is essentially a two-year contract and it is up to the chairman or the ranking member to put together their staffs. The challenge, as I discussed earlier, was made even more difficult by the fact that our staff was cut in half. We were about to go into a session that would require so much, but we were expected to do it with less staff and a lot of new faces. The first thing I had to do was to start building a team that would work together and take to the dais as a unified group. It was against that backdrop that we met on a bright and cold winter day in January to begin the process of uniting.

The members of the committee on the Republican side brought many talents to the fight. We had legends on our side like Jim Sensenbrenner, a former chairman of the committee who had led the committee in the aftermath of 9/11. We had veterans of the committee like Steve Chabot from Ohio, who had served on the Clinton impeachment team. We had fighters like Louie Gohmert, Jim Jordan, John Ratcliffe, Mike Johnson, Matt Gaetz, Ken Buck, Martha Roby, and Andy Biggs. Then we were able to bring on to the committee new members who were committed to fighting for the Republican ideas we all cared about. Some of the new committee members were veteran Representatives who came from other committees, great folks such as Tom McKlintock and Debbie Lesko. We filled out the committee with four freshman: Ben Cline, Kelly Armstrong, Greg Stuebe, and Guy Reshenthaler. This was a strong group of members who recognized that they would be front row to the biggest battles in this Congress. I told them during that first organizational meeting that I believed we were in for a fight with the Democrats, who had shown no desire to work with us on anything, even down to staff decisions about whom we could keep. The battlefield was set, and we set out on how we were going to attack.

The general feeling on our side was that we needed to go forward at every opportunity and not give an inch when it came to the circus that was ahead. When you are in the minority, it is not a matter of whether you will win in the traditional sense of winning because you will not. They have the votes and can win on any motion. However, it was my sense that Chairman Nadler was so focused on pushing his agenda and proving that he was the right one for the job of leading the committee that he failed to realize that much of what he wanted to do was purely political. You see, you can win a vote but lose the story. We had every intention of making them lose the story and the messaging on all their initiatives and not just the relentless attacks on the president. If we could keep reminding the American people that the policies put forth by the Democrats were out of step and dangerous we could help fashion the story to reflect that although they came in saying they wanted to do things to help people, at the core of their message were nothing more than hatred for Donald Trump and a liberal wish list of ideas ranging from gun control and voting rights bills to abortion expansion and immigration policy that would simply open our borders and make the situation worse instead of better on our southern border. In order to make our case and, at every opportunity, take away the majority's numerical advantage, we would be smarter and more direct in our messaging.

I laid the strategy out in our organizational meeting with the members. The main theme was that if the Democrats had no real intention of governing or using the committee as it should, then we had one goal: give Chairman Nadler no easy breaths. My goal was to make sure that when the Democrats got up each morning, they were thinking, *What they are up to today?* To fight when you do not have the votes, you have to be smart and use what is given to you. We determined that we would use every proper procedural and substantive parliamentary maneuver we could to help make our points and give us the opportunity to shape the debate that would occur in our committee. What we thought at the time but was not confirmed until we started the hearings was that Chairman Nadler and his staff had thought about many things, but actually running the meetings of the committee was not one of them. Chairman Nadler, for all his skill as a legislator, was not one to be bothered by things such as proper parliamentary procedure. It would be the Achilles' heel that we used over and over to frustrate the majority and show the American people that the Democrats were not about governing the country.

At the organizational meeting, I made it clear as we went through each area of the committee's work that I wanted them to think of ways to ensure we would have a fair hearing and that when it came time for markups of bills they would have an opportunity to offer amendments that, even if not accepted by the majority, would force them to have to take votes that put them in positions of defending untenable ideas, which would allow people to see what priorities the Democrats really had. The other part of our plan was to make good use and encourage the members or our committee to take advantage of every media opportunity they had. Our communications staff was to make sure that our members were out spreading the message that we had the better ideas and the Democrats were simply carrying out a plan that would harm not help our country.

Members of Congress are not typically shy individuals and are able to express themselves to their voters back home; otherwise, they would not get elected. I must say, however, that one of the best assets we had in the 116th Congress on the Republican side of the Judiciary Committee was members who knew how to communicate. As the year progressed, members such as Matt Gaetz, Jim Jordan, John Ratcliffe, Andy Biggs, and Mike Johnson became household names. Their passion and fire were so effective that rarely did a meeting happen in the committee in which some member on the Democrat side of the aisle was not complaining about something that one of us had said the night or the week before.

The constant exposure gave us a platform that helped people understand what was going on, even when the print media and the Washington mainstream media would downplay or belittle our work on the committee. It also helped that we had the backing of the president, who would often tweet about what was going on with our members and the attacks by the Democrats on him. President Trump, probably more than any modern president, understood that when he went straight to the people via his social media presence, he could shape the message and force the media to shape their message around whatever he wanted to talk about. It was a good combination: members who could communicate and a president who could back us up and emphasize to the American people the craziness that was about to overtake the committee.

The morning of February 8, 2019, should have been a normal Friday morning, with members taking final votes and then doing the usual dash from the Hill to the airport. Committee hearings are not typically held on Fridays. In fact, if any are held at all, they are hearings that are not particularly important and that we could not find time on the calendar for earlier in the week. But this Friday was special. It was the first of what we on the Republican side did not realize would be a regular occurring theme of the Judiciary Committee, what I would come to refer to as Popcorn Hearings. They were hearings that really were not designed to get an answer to a burning question or even to enlighten the audience or the committee on some pressing issue. No, the purpose of these hearings was to bring different witnesses, some administration officials or others, before the committee to be harassed if they were with the administration or if they were not part of the administration. They were there to say how bad the Trump administration was for the country.

On this day, the chairman fulfilled his promise to bring the Acting Attorney General Matt Whitaker to testify supposedly for the purpose of an Oversight Hearing on the Department of Justice. The real reason was that they thought they could get the attorney general to give up information about what they thought was their goose with the golden egg, Robert Mueller and his investigation into Donald Trump.

To understand the desire of the Democrats and Chairman Nadler, you must understand that they were not really concerned about the Department of Justice and its operations. They were only concerned with Mueller and ensuring that even in his limited time as head of the Department of Justice, Matt Whitaker would not do anything to harm the investigation that they were convinced would lead to President Trump's downfall. If you had any doubts about the true intentions, I just remind you that less than a week from this supposed blockbuster hearing, William Barr would be sworn in as the attorney general of the United States after his Senate confirmation. The Democrats had never liked Whitaker. In fact, the State of Maryland filed a lawsuit in federal court that argued that Whitaker was not qualified to be attorney general and that he was a partisan hack. Even Democratic senators got involved. Sens. Blumenthal (D-CT), Hirono (D-HI), and Whitehouse (D-RI) argued that the appointment was illegal, but at the root of every argument about Matt Whitaker was the determination by the Democrats that everything that Donald Trump was doing was an attempt to derail the Mueller report. But as the hearing showed, seeing the president behind all your made-up conspiracy theories does not make it so.

The hearing kicked off that morning against the backdrop of staged drama dealing with the issuance of a subpoena the day before by Chairman Nadler. The chairman always wanted the hearings to look more ominous than they really were. He would threaten to subpoena everyone, even those who were willing to come without one. The problem was that Chairman Nadler thought the subpoena issuance was a great optic to give a sense of legitimacy to his show hearings. The reality is that Acting Attorney General Whitaker was more than willing to come without a subpoena.

In fact, he was looking forward to coming. I had met with him in his conference room at the Department of Justice before the hearing. It was a good meeting in which I found him to be very laid-back. He seemed to be enjoying the job. While sitting in the conference room that had been the office of Robert Kennedy when he was attorney general, you could sense the history and the power the room held. Attorney General Whitaker was seated at the end of the conference table in a chair that was not designed for a big Iowa Hawkeye football player. As he talked, I could see him lean back and move in his chair, and I worried that it might give way. He even laughed at one point, saying the chairs around the table lacked a little for folks like him. I took away from that meeting that he was honored to serve the department and President Trump in his role. He had a real desire to talk about the things the department was working on and the hopes for the future. He truly did seem to understand that he was given a great opportunity, and he wanted to be remembered as doing a good job. The Democrats were scared he would interfere with Mueller, but in the end, he did his job and endured the criticism. As we left that night from the conference room, I looked over at the picture of William Barr from when he had served previously as attorney general. His presence in that room was felt, although I have to admit at the time I did not realize how much the new attorney general would be at the center of the hurricane that was to come. Unfortunately, the Democrats were only in the mood to attack Matt and portray him as nothing more than a lackey for the president.

In committee hearings, the format is pretty much the same no matter what is going to happen that day. The chairman calls the hearing to order and then proceeds to give what is known as an opening statement. The chairman goes first and lays out what they believe the hearing will show. In this case, it was just a further push against the administration and the obsession with the Mueller investigation. As the chairman came into the room, it was everything that they wanted. They room was filled, the networks were carrying the hearing live, and the press tables were overflowing. The space in front of the witness table was packed like a mosh pit at a rock concert, with every camera charged and clicking photos of all the excitement. The room ebbed and flowed with excitement before the hearing. When members came in, the cameras would start their chatter. Then, the acting attorney general entered with his associates, and the room was at a fever pitch. This was the first big hearing under the Democrats' control. The feeling you got from talking to some of my colleagues on the Democratic side was this was not just a hearing to provide oversight of the Department of Justice, but it was also the first in keeping its promise to the base that elected them and allowed the House to flip control to them. They knew that their voters were not fans of this administration, and this was for them. They would be the tip of the spear pushing back on President Trump, and if they were fortunate, the Mueller investigation would give them the evidence they needed to impeach the president. But for now, that was all in the future. Now they had to deliver. The show was about to start.

As Chairman Nadler began his opening statement, it did not take long to get at the real reason for the hearing: Mueller. Chairman Nadler rehashed discussions from December during which Whitaker had said he was not obligated to excuse himself from the oversight of the Mueller investigation. In fact, for all that was said this day by the Democrats about the acting attorney general, the one thing that came out was that, contrary to the dire predictions of the Democrats about Whitaker, he did not interfere in the Mueller investigation and never refused a request from the investigation. He was combative and, for the most part, kept his composure even in the face of the personal attack that was on display by the Democrats.

After the chairman finished his opening statement, he recognized me for my opening statement. I must admit that, for just a moment right before speaking, I had to take a deep breath and hold back emotion of my own. It had been over thirty years since I was first in Washington, DC, interning for my hometown congressman, Ed Jenkins, and here I was, about to give an opening statement in a packed hearing room as the ranking member of the Judiciary Committee. As I looked out over the audience, I was thankful for the opportunity laid before me. I have often said in describing myself that I am just a state trooper's kid from North Georgia. My wife, Lisa, and I had sacrificed a lot for this time to serve. I was a long way from home, but home was not all that far from me as I thought about my wife and family. It was in that moment, in a year that would eventually be filled with many moments, that I thought of my mom, who had passed away in June of the previous year. I had come a long way to have a front seat to history, and for all those who had placed their trust in me, I was going to give it my all.

I realized that with all the emphasis of the Democrats and especially the chairman to appear tough when the reality was anything but, it was up to me to call the hearing what it was—a farce. This was not a hearing to gain information but a chance to attack a witness who agreed to come. A witness who, as you could tell from the questions that would come, they felt was beneath them. They did not like that he was in the position he was in, and they disliked even more that he felt the president was doing a good job. In what would become my role in the hearings as we went forward, I was going lay out the truth as we recognized it on our side, and I was going to wake up the crowd if I had to. If the Democrats were going to use their time to parade around in veiled and not-so-veiled threats against anyone who disagreed with them, I was going to point out the hypocrisy. They wanted to say they had forced Whitaker to appear that morning, but I pointed out that they had caved just the night before. He was not there because of a subpoena. The wasted energy of the previous day was lost by a chairman so concerned with losing the moment in the media that he caved on his threats against the attorney general and allowed him to come without a compulsion of subpoena. It was all about the show, and I was going to call it out. *Newsweek* reporter Jason Le Miere wrote that in my opening statement, I launched into an incredible tirade against the hearing:

"This hearing is pointless," Collins said. "If this is the way we're going to go, if this is where we're going then we'll have plenty of stunts, we're going to have plenty of theatrics. Bring your popcorn. I am thinking about maybe we set up a popcorn machine at the back because this is what it's become. It's become a show."

After the hearing was over, Fox News Reporter Chad Pergram came up to me and asked me if I was serious about getting a popcorn machine. At first, I laughed and just sort of blew off the question, and then said that I would think about it. A few weeks later, we took up donations, and we bought a popcorn machine that to this day still sits in the minority staff room next door to the Judiciary hearing room. At every big show hearing after that first one with Whitaker the staff would fire up the popcorn machine, and the smell of popcorn would waft through the hearing room. It was my way of reminding the Democrats that if they wanted to put on a show without real results, we would pop the popcorn and participate, knowing that the only thing that we were accomplishing was raising TV ratings, but as far as helping the American people, we were a long way from that. The clock and the calendar were just beginning their push. But even then, you could tell this committee had an intentional meeting with destiny, and the Democrats were hell-bent on getting there.

Over the next few weeks, Washington, and the rest of the world it seemed, played the parlor game of guessing when the Mueller report was going to be released and, when it was, what it was going to say about the president.

To understand this faith placed in the investigation by the Democrats and the media elites and, frankly, some Republicans, you must understand the persona and legend that is Robert Mueller. Robert Mueller was going to be the person who could bring it all together, and when he was done, he would solve all these problems and bring to justice those who had done wrong. So, to understand why the Democrats felt this way about a man known by many to be a conservative Republican, you have to understand the persona that Robert Mueller carried when he was named by Deputy Attorney General Rod Rosenstein, who was overseeing the Russia investigation since the recusal of Attorney General Jeff Sessions. The recusal by Jeff Sessions will go down as one of the strangest and worst decisions. Instead of standing up and being the attorney general, Sessions not only allowed the very ones attacking the president to clear him out of the way of doing his job, but he then allowed the proverbial foxes into the hen house because those who wanted to take down the president the most were now left to run the show. And with the firing of James Comey, they got what they wanted: a special counsel to investigate the president of the United States. So, while Sessions looked on, his deputy, Rod Rosenstein, decided to bring back a man who had an almost mythic standing in Washington, DC, when it came to work ethic and integrity—Robert Mueller. But what he could not have known at the time was that Robert Mueller was not the Mueller of old, and the team of partisans that he surrounded himself with in his investigation were about to go down a very long and expensive path that was more sound and fury than anything else. They thought they had what they wanted, but in the end, the one who knew he was innocent, Donald Trump, was shown to have been right all along. So begins the Mueller investigation.

Robert Mueller was one of those individuals that if you looked at his life and service, you would believe that the character Mr. Smith, who came to Washington, or Atticus Finch from *To Kill a Mockingbird*, who fought against injustice no matter the odds, was brought to life in one man. Robert Mueller went to Princeton and, after graduating, joined the Marines and headed out for Vietnam. In Vietnam, Robert Mueller distinguished himself with his bravery and leadership. He was awarded the Bronze Star with Valor for his actions on the battlefield. He always believed that he was lucky to have made it out of Vietnam. He had seen so much death, and he believed that since he made it out, he should give back to the society and country he loved. When he left the Marine Corps, he attended University of Virginia Law School. Over the next forty years, Robert Mueller was in and out of private practice and working for the Department of Justice. It was however his appointment by President George Bush to be the head of the FBI that brought his prominence to the country as a whole. He was sworn in just one week before the country was attacked on 9/11. He was the FBI director for almost all the Bush administration and served four years for President Obama. It was from this office that he oversaw making sure that the FBI was vigilant to not let another terrorist attack happen. However, it was his reputation as a straight, by-the-book player that prompted some high-profile disagreements with the Bush-Cheney team, especially when it came to the use of data-collection techniques and enhanced interrogation techniques used on foreign fighters. I first got to know the director right after I got to Congress, during the Boston Marathon bomber case. He would come and address Congress about that event, and then, later, I would get to know him, as he would come and testify before the House Judiciary Committee on FBI oversight. Most of the members of the committee and those in Congress had a generally good opinion of Mueller—everyone except Congressman Louie Gohmert, who often would clash with the director over issues in the FBI. That clash would last all the way through the Mueller report and hearing.

Robert Mueller also had the reputation of being exceptionally good as a witness before Congress. Some people come before Congress and think they can wing it. Others come overthinking it or, worse, with an agenda to make the members look bad. I can assure you that if a witness tries that tack of attacking the questioner, it usually does not end very well. Mueller had mastered what we called the Mueller treatment. If he did not like a line of questioning or thought the member was being unfair to him or the department, his answers would get short and very much to the point. Then he would give what I had been told was the Mueller stare. It was a stare that said to the member, "I have answered your question, and you will not get any more out of me." That stare became famous and had shut down more than one member of the House and the Senate who he felt had abused their time. All in all, most who knew Robert Mueller before this investigation would have said he was the perfect choice to lead the investigation. What no one knew was this was not the Mueller of old and the investigation had taken on the appearance of a runaway exercise that was out of control.

From day one, the president did not like the fact that Mueller had been appointed as a special counsel. He viewed it as a partisan witch hunt that was only going on for one reason, and that was not to find the truth but to attack and harass him as president. He also realized that the use of the special counsel was a predicate for all the conversations about him being impeached. In many conversations with the president, he would make it clear that the investigation was a sham and that it should not be going on. However, he never did anything to impede or stop the investigation. As much as he did not like it and expressed those thoughts, he continued to do his job. I knew from talking with him that he did not want to be impeached. He did not want that to be attached to his presidency. But as I shared with him, after the election of 2018, if the Democrats were willing to take the political heat and bring articles of impeachment, there was really nothing we in the minority could do except keep pounding them for the stupidity and foolishness of their actions. As long as the Mueller investigation was ongoing, the Democrats could hide behind the report and make any claim they wanted about the investigation. But in the end, when the report was released, their greatest fears were realized: Donald Trump had not done anything wrong, and no matter how they spun it the game was up.

But before that conclusion was reached, Chairman Nadler had to keep his committee members occupied fulfilling the promises they had made to their liberal base. Over the next month, we took up bills such as the inappropriately named Equality Act, which raised some serious questions about gender and the effects of legalizing what for many on our side was a destruction of gender as we know it. We also took up what has always been a desire of the Democrats: a continued attack on the Second Amendment. They did not have the votes for a complete ban on "assault rifles," which is the term for firearms they do not like. But we considered HR 8, a gun bill dealing with background checks. Much can be written about this bill, and much has, but it goes without saying that nothing in this bill would stop the mass shootings that they want to stop. In fact, as our members kept pointing out the obvious in the hearing on the bill—that the bill would not have stopped any loss of life at Parkland, Aurora, or Sandy Hook—the Democrats seemed flustered. The talking points that they kept repeating were being met with not just resistance from Republicans but the truth about what they were trying to sell. But when Art Acevedo, the chief of police from Houston, Texas, finally stated out of exasperation that he acknowledged that the bill might not have worked in those situations but that if it just saved one life it would be worth it, it was just what the battered Democrats needed. Every member on their side began to repeat that talking point given to them by a witness. It can be tough when your talking points don't match reality, but they kept pressing on, believing that they had to do something, even though they knew that it would not do anything to solve the problem they cared so much about.

The real reason, however, for focusing on these hearings is not the bills that they brought up. Rather, it was the complete breakdown that was occurring in how the committee was functioning or, better yet, not functioning. Chairman Nadler was not good at running the mechanics of a hearing or a markup. I bring this up to not disparage the chairman but to point out what became a huge problem in trying to get anything done in the committee. Chairman Nadler was never one known for patience. He has been in Congress a long time. He is part of what most would agree was the old guard. He is much more comfortable reading the stacks of papers that he would bring to the committee room than paying close attention to the proceedings. I found, in my time sitting next to him, that he was also easily distracted, whether by something that got his attention from his ever-present stack of papers or by someone asking him a question. He would go on and on about whatever attracted his attention, at times oblivious to the goings-on around him. The problem was not him being distracted in regular hearings, but it was his complete lack of bearing when it came to hearings in which there was controversy, especially in markups. This disregard for the rules of the committee started coming to light in these hearings in February and March 2019 and would continue throughout the year, causing what should have been easily solved problems to become full-blown issues.

The inability to run the committee ran headlong into our desire to enforce the rights of the minority. The US House of Representatives is a place in which the majority has complete control. They control the committees, what bills will be voted on, and what amendments are to be offered and when. The majority controls the schedule of when members will be in Washington and when they will be back in their districts. I am often frustrated by members, including those in my own party who believe that they can control the outcomes in the House. It is just not right for a member of the minority to tell his or her constituents that they will get something done if it is not a priority of the majority. You can advocate for your ideas and work hard to get them into the plans of the majority, but at the end of the day, whether Republican or Democrat, the majority's will can put a swift and hard end to the best of ideas from the minority. The one equalizer is that rules are in place to protect the minority's right to be heard. That is it: we have the right to be heard and to use the rules of the House to make amendments and prolong debate, but that is about it. It is when the rights of the minority are shut out that you see tensions rise in the House. The tension was already palpable in the Judiciary Committee, as we in the minority were having to endure the hearings aimed only at trying to disparage the president and have markups on bills such as gun control that went against our very core beliefs. We knew that we would not win in the end, but it was our right to offer amendments and have debate as long as we could. This is where the trouble started. Chairman Nadler, supported by his members on the committee, did not want to seem to be bothered with listening to the complaints of the minority. The chairman would comment on Republican amendments or disparage members' points as being foolish or outrageous. This is a break in decorum, which began to overflow into his members of the committee. The members would see the chairman's action and were empowered to act out on their own, knowing it would not get called out.

Basic fairness is something that we should all try for in working on a committee, but it is a must for the chairman. What starts off as allowing his members to go too long in their questioning just because the chairman likes their questions while on the other side shutting down a member of the minority as soon as their time is up begins to cause friction. The adage that motion causes friction could not have been more in view as hearing after hearing and markup after markup, the rules were abused to put down and punish the minority. I spent most of my time having to fight with the chairman on behalf of my members for the rules to be applied fairly. We would point out the rules that were being violated, and they would look at us and say we can do what we want. Jon Ferro was my parliamentarian and counsel on the committee. He was an expert at the rules and could quote chapter and verse of our House and committee rules. Jon would have to spend more time trying to keep the majority in line than anything else. The fight got so bad that during the markups, the committee would just completely break down into shouting matches because Chairman Nadler would refuse to follow the rules and was determined to shut the minority down and get on with what he wanted to accomplish.

This was on complete display during the markup on HR 8, the gun control legislation. Chairman Nadler made it noticeably clear at the beginning of the hearing that we would finish that day and that nothing we did would stop him. As I stated earlier, the minority has very few options when it comes to trying to influence legislation. One way that the minority can participate is by offering and debating amendments. I can assure you that this bill was not popular with the Republican members of the committee, and we had prepared over one hundred amendments for the bill. I had tried to warn the majority that they ought to schedule more time for the markup, but they were determined to move forward and finish in the time allotted. This was frustrating to me because this is the same majority that had spent only four years in the majority since 1993. They had used everything they could to influence bills, knowing that they would lose but knowing it was all they had to work with and if it made the majority uncomfortable or frustrated, so be it because that was the way the game was played. It was especially frustrating to those of us on the Judiciary Committee, who for many years had watched the Democrats offer motion after motion, amendment after amendment, and move to strike the last word to keep debate going more times than we could count, and Chairman Goodlatte would sit there and let them do it even when many on our side wanted him to end it. It was the discretion shown by Chairman Goodlatte that I thought would have been shared by Chairman Nadler. It was not. He was going to get things done so he could move on to other things, and he and his senior staff were not going to bend. During the markup, the chairman let it slip on more than one occasion that he we would finish tonight and that he was not going to tolerate our useless and deleterious amendments.

The Democrats had a problem, however. The Democrat staff, in their haste to get the bill marked up, forgot to include a motion in the nature of a substitute that would have allowed them to end debate. Since they rushed the bill forward and did not have the amendment in the nature of a substitute, we had every right to keep offering amendments until we got tired. After the chairman complained about the number of amendments and threatened to shut us down, I reminded the chairman that he could not do that due to the way the bill was presented. Let me just assure you that did not go over very well. Their staff pitched a fit, but Jon calmly reminded them and showed them the rules, and they were trapped. They then had to make plans to try and offer an amendment in the nature of a substitute, but the damage was already done. What transpired in that markup and other hearings during this time forced me to write a letter to the chairman outlining his egregious behavior and asking that he change his ways or I was going to have to appeal his behavior to the House as a whole on the floor.

I wish I could say that over the course of the year it got better, but the best that I can say is that Chairman Nadler's inability to run a committee meeting not only frustrated us but his own members and leadership. When the Judiciary Committee was breaking down so badly, the message that they were trying to get out was lost. We benefited from the poor leadership because other members could see that we were running circles around them, and people were talking. The organizational meeting at which we had spoken of using every opportunity to enforce the rules and every procedural option open to us was proving invaluable. The perception was quickly becoming that the committee was out of control, and even when bills got out, the message of the bills was lost in the poor presentation. The majority was struggling, and it was all their fault. Poor management of the committee and the tunnel vision focus on the Mueller investigation were beginning to show.

I did not realize at the time that these hearings, which were painful to go through, were a precursor of things that would occur later in the year when impeachment started, and the committee of impeachment was sidelined. In looking back on these events, I can understand why most Americans are fed up with Washington and why someone like Donald Trump, who spoke straight from the heart, was so appealing to so many. The American people are an understanding bunch. They are willing to put up with a lot if they know that at the end of the day, it will help them. All they were seeing out of Washington was fighting for the sake of fighting with nothing truly getting done.

And their impressions weren't wrong. In March 2019, the committee was in disarray. The majority spent all their time waiting on the Mueller report. They did nothing else except attack the president. For example, as we waited, the committee, whose jurisdiction included immigration, largely ignored the exploding problem of unaccompanied minors on our southern border. Further, the rancor and discord between members began to hit a fever pitch. And the can of gasoline that would push the fire higher was about to be tipped over.

The Mueller report, which had taken over two years and millions of dollars to complete, was about to be released. Each player in the story had their own idea about what would happen when the report was released. The Democrats saw the report as their ticket to get rid of President Trump. They had banked the entire Congress and the upcoming presidential election on it. The Republicans believed that it would show what we all thought, and that it would not be bad for the president. They also believed the report would reveal that their previous investigations into the Department of Justice were vindicated. They believed that the report would show those bad actors for what they were: subversive. Then you had the one at the heart of the report, President Donald Trump. He was furious over the investigation, and just as the temperatures of spring were rising in Washington, the president was more than ready to put this behind him. He knew he had done nothing wrong, and he wanted to world to know it. But he did not trust Robert Mueller, and the waiting was getting to everybody.

There has been a lot of discussion over the past year about the president and the lead-up to the Mueller report. President Trump was very engaged in what was going on in Congress. It was not unusual to get a call from the president after one of the hearings to discuss the proceedings and to wonder what the Democrats were up to next. Contrary to what the mainstream media would have you believe, President Trump wanted only one thing, and that was to do a good job for the American people and to make our country better. He felt, as many of us did, that he was never given a fair chance by the media and the Democrats after he won the presidency. All you need to look at is reports that said his inauguration day was the beginning of the countdown to impeachment. Let that sink in a minute. He had not been sworn into office one day, and the media was already predicting impeachment. He was never given any kind of a honeymoon to work on things. Instead, he was met with scorn and disdain from the media and the Democrats on the Hill. This continued in everything he was trying to do in his first few months. In fact, he did not even have a complete cabinet until almost May 2017 because of the delays in the US Senate in confirming his appointments. It was the attacks that were out of his control that caused him the most frustration. When I became ranking member of the Judiciary Committee, I was also put in the position of being the lead Republican in defense against the many unfounded attacks on the president. The president knew that they were out to get him, but he kept working and fumed about the attacks. He did not want to be impeached. He did not feel he had done anything wrong, and he felt that the Mueller investigation was nothing more than Democrat attacking him because they did not like him and because he had beat the left's hero, Hillary Clinton. As we prepared behind the scenes for the eventual release of Mueller's report, we knew that not just what we did in the committee would be watched, but also that how we handled what came out would impact the president and his agenda. I had worked closely with him and

Jared Kushner on the First Step Act, the most comprehensive criminal justice reform passed in decades. I knew his passion to help people and this country. But I also knew that once the report came out, it would be the only thing discussed and, depending on what it said, would determine if the Democrats would get their wish and have what they believed would be enough to impeach this president they despised so much.

CHAPTER 2:

THE MUELLER REPORT

March 24, 2019, was the date that the world had been anxiously waiting for. Attorney General Bill Barr announced a summary of the findings in the Mueller report. As one of the people delegated to get briefed on the report, I knew the day would come, but just like everyone else, I did not know when it would come or how it would be disseminated. The order for the special counsel simply said the report would be given to the attorney general and then it would be up to him to decide when and how the report's findings would be released.

Our staff had been preparing since the first of the year for the time that the investigation was complete and the report ready for release to the attorney general. As 2019 progressed from winter to spring, we did not feel that the report would bring any more indictments than had already been filed. Members of the team were dispersing, and of the ones that were left, it was reported that they were simply putting the final details on the report. The real question was what the report would include as far as reports of collusion among the Trump campaign and Russia, but some of us were also concerned about whether the investigators investigated what we on the Republican side of the Hill were upset about: the flimsy and careless way these investigations had started to begin with. How could we be still looking into the president and the administration when we knew that the whole premise of the investigation was started not on solid investigative research but on a dossier that was full of holes and outright distortions? The Republican members of the Judiciary Committee who had been investigating felt strongly that the investigation should have focused as well on these things.

In the months leading up to the Mueller report becoming public, I had decided that I was going to release the transcripts of the interviews that had been conducted by the joint committee work of the Judiciary Committee and the Oversight Committee. These transcripts were in our possession, and, of course, the committees that were now in Democrat control had no interest in releasing them. I felt, however, that the American people should know what folks like Jim Comey, Peter Strzok, Nellie Ohr, Bruce Ohr, and Andrew McCabe had said under oath to members of the committee. In releasing these transcripts, the press and the American people would be able to see for themselves the problems that were uncovered by the investigation. We decided that the best way to release these transcripts would be by announcing the release on the House floor and providing a link for people to go and read for themselves. So, on March 8, 2019, I went to the well on the House floor and made the Bruce Ohr transcript available.

For those who watch CSPAN, you will be familiar with a part of the day called one-minute speeches. It is during this time you can talk about pretty much whatever you want to talk about. Members use the time to highlight legislation that will be voted on that week or introduce bills that they have written. The one minutes are also used by members to recognize constituents back home for the amazing accomplishments in their lives. The time can also be more somber, such as when we go to the floor to eulogize friends and neighbors back home. These are sleepy times on the floor when members come down with their speech, typically written out by staff to make sure that we stay within the one-minute deadline. You quite often see members talking and joking with each other during this time sometimes even trying to get a fellow member to laugh or otherwise get distracted during their time. It is one of those times that you get to see the humanity of the members of Congress. It was one of those normal days in March when I went to the floor to begin the release of these transcripts. I remember sitting down to wait my turn. Another member asked me what I was going to talk about, and I just smiled and said, "You may want to stick around for this one minute." When I got into the well and announced my intentions, you could feel a change on the floor. As I looked up, Democratic members, who were waiting to give their one-minutes, raised their heads and began to whisper to one another. When I announced that I would be releasing the Bruce Ohr transcript and yielded the well, you could hear and feel the excited buzz on the floor. Some thought that what I had done was improper; some may have thought it to be illegal. In spite of what anyone thought, it was entirely proper, and judging by the hits to the site, all of them had their staff download the transcript. We were no longer going to sit silently and wait for the Mueller investigation. It was time to go on offense, and this was a direct shot.

I continued to release the transcripts, much to the frustration of Chairman Nadler. We were on the offense after having to endure the constant barrage of anti-Trump rhetoric that emerged in almost every hearing or markup that the committee undertook. I genuinely believe that if we had a hearing on any issue, it would be turned into something that the president had done or was something that Democrats thought he might be doing. The level of distrust and bitterness directed at President Trump did not level off, and the fact that I was releasing transcripts that showed what many of us felt was the bias at the Department of Justice and specifically the FBI did not fit their narrative. They just dug in even more and waited for the release of the Mueller report. It was all they cared about because they just knew that this was going to be the golden ticket to get rid of a man that they could not stand to see in the White House. So as the days passed by, they were getting more impatient. Privately, some shared with me that they thought the report would be a bust and they would be in the unenviable position of having to convince their base and the world that no matter what it said, it was bad for Donald Trump. I have often said that the best way to get out of a hole is to quit digging. It was rather humorous to watch the Democrats as they kept digging the hole of dependence on the Mueller report. Instead of putting down the shovel, they kept ordering more. What they did not know was that their day of reckoning was just around the corner. The Mueller report was coming, and soon the world would see that what they thought was the end for the president was really the beginning of a free fall of spin to keep the story alive.

As we waited for the report to be delivered to the attorney general, we were trying to be prepared for how to respond to the results. It was interesting to listen to the many pundits who were making the rounds describing the release of the report and how it should be done. Some indicated that the report would be released by Mueller in a grand press conference or dumped online in its entirety like the famous Starr Report from the Clinton impeachment saga. The reality was far from that dramatic. Since the Clinton administration, the special prosecutor position was allowed to expire and was not revived by Congress. The part that most had missed that under the order that Deputy Attorney General Rod Rosenstein used to set forth was that it would use the following for guidance: Sections 600.4 through 600.10 of Title 28 of the Code of Federal Regulations are applicable to the special counsel. It is the standard that the special counsel was to use to guide his work, including how he would give his findings to the attorney general, William Barr.

§ 600.9 Notification and reports by the Attorney General.

(a) The Attorney General will notify the Chairman and Ranking Minority Member of the Judiciary Committees of each House of Congress, with an explanation for each action -

(1) Upon appointing a Special Counsel.

(2) Upon removing any Special Counsel; and

(3) Upon conclusion of the Special Counsel's investigation, including, to the extent consistent with applicable law, a description and explanation of instances (if any) in which the Attorney General concluded that

a proposed action by a Special Counsel was so inappropriate or unwarranted under established Departmental practices that it should not be pursued.

(b) The notification requirement in paragraph (a)(1) of this section may be tolled by the Attorney General upon a finding that legitimate investigative or privacy concerns require confidentiality. At such time as confidentiality is no longer needed, the notification will be provided.

(c) *The Attorney General may determine that public release of these reports would be in the public interest, to the extent that release would comply with applicable legal restrictions.* All other releases of information by any Department of Justice employee, including the Special Counsel and staff, concerning matters handled by Special Counsels shall be governed by the generally applicable Departmental guidelines concerning public comment with respect to any criminal investigation, and relevant law.

§ 600.8 Notification and reports by the Special Counsel.

(c) *Closing documentation.* **At the conclusion of the Special Counsel's work, he or she shall provide the Attorney General with a confidential report explaining the prosecution or declination decisions reached by the Special Counsel.**

These are the applicable code sections that would govern the release of the special counsel's findings. After studying these sections, we were struck with the fact that at the end of the day, all the special counsel had to report to the attorney general was a confidential, not public, report that explained only prosecution or declination decisions reached by the investigation. It should be noted that it does not keep the special counsel from giving more information to the attorney general about the investigation. But at its heart, Robert Mueller would have been well within the rules to have just given the bare minimum to Bill Barr. It is also worth noting that the attorney general only had to notify the House and Senate Judiciary Committee chairmen and ranking members of the ending of the reports and the actions taken. It is also clear that, contrary to what the world of the media and the Democrats were building up as this grand presentation of a report from Robert Mueller, its presentation ultimately would depend on what the special counsel chose to give and what the attorney general chose to make public.

At the end of the day, it was up to Bill Barr to decide what he would release. To the attorney general's credit, when asked about the release of the report, he stated that he would release as much as he could, with the hope of releasing it all within the bounds of security and privacy. In trying to find out what the attorney general had in mind as far as a release, our staff talked and I spoke with the attorney general, and the response was that, by statute, we would be notified as required. This led to some interesting discussions in our office about how much time we would have to read and digest what would be coming out, what we thought might be in the report, and finally just how much would we be dealing with, not only in the size of the report but also its scope.

So as the world prepared for a big public spectacle, we tried to tamp down the expectations on our side. We let each of our members on the committee know that as soon as we were notified, we would let them know and would disseminate all the information we had to them. We also tried to say that we were not sure what the information would look like. I did not want our members to be expecting one thing and get surprised by the results. All that was left was for Mueller to deliver his report and the attorney general to decide when or if he would release the report to the world. The wait was on, and the most overused parlor game in Washington was "When is it going to be released?"

The team was on call. We had gotten what we believed was an indication that an announcement was soon. The report had been delivered to the attorney general. Now we were just waiting to find out when we would know what was going to be put out. I flew home that week from Washington feeling a mix of excitement and anxiety. We were prepared as best we could as a team, and we had been in contact with our members on the committee. We knew that we would want everyone to be on message and on media as soon as we could get out there. The Democrats had become increasingly impatient, and, frankly, Chairman Nadler and others were getting edgy. When we would talk on the dais, just the two of us, you could sense the frustration in his voice. Nadler was personally frustrated because of the very contentious start to the Congress, with him and me constantly clashing over his style, or lack of it, in running the committee. Additionally, it was apparent that, despite all the bluster about how the Mueller report would deliver what Nadler and other Democrats were hoping for, you could see that they were not only scared of what the report would actually say, they were also scared of what their reaction would be. You see, when you put everything into a report, you have to accept the good and the bad. And right now, the Democrats had no idea what that report was going to say. They hoped that it would be the very tool to achieve their goal of getting rid of Donald Trump and all that he stands; they had talked about it and talked about it and talked about it so much that they had really convinced themselves that the Mueller report was going to be the magic bullet. The problem was that they just did not know. So, their waiting continued, not knowing what was going to happen yet hoping for the best. So as their waiting continued and the crankiness built, the world waited for what Bill Barr was going to do.

When I woke up on March 24, it was just another normal Sunday. I did not think about the report all that much, and normal activities in the Collins house were in full swing. My family and I went together to church and were filling the day with activities around the house. I was grilling on the back deck, and it was going to be just a good day with good food and a little time with the family. I needed to run to the grocery store for a few last-minute items for the grill, so I left the house and headed off, not knowing that by the time I returned, the world would be on edge. Today was the day that Bill Barr was releasing what would come to be known as the four-page summary of the Mueller report, and it was the beginning of the next phase of the Democrats' crusade to find something that could be used to impeach Donald Trump.

When you are all over the media, people tend to recognize you, and in my hometown, where I have lived for fifty-four years, people would often come up and ask me about what was going on in Congress and what was happening with the Mueller report. So sometimes, when I go to the grocery store, I plug my earphones into my phone and listen to music while buying my groceries and getting in and out as quickly as possible. My wife has learned to understand that a simple trip to the grocery store, or anywhere in town for that matter, could take anywhere from five minutes to an hour. I did not mind really because one of the things that is missing in our government today is accessibility to our elected officials. And for me, I always tried to take the time to talk to folks no matter what I might be up to. That was what was happening on this Sunday. Little did I know that about the time I got into the grocery store and started walking around, I was about to receive a call that would change everything.

When my phone buzzed, I looked and saw it was Brendan Belair. Brendan was the staff director for the committee, and he had been with me my entire time in Congress, previously as my chief of staff. So, it was not unusual to get a call from Brendan, even on a Sunday. Brendan alerted me that he had been put on thirty-minute notice to get to the office because the attorney general was about to deliver by hand his statement on the Mueller report. Of course, I asked if he had any idea what was in the report. He did not. All he knew was that he needed to be in the office and that the statement would be delivered there. So, he called the rest of the staff, and we planned to reconvene as soon as the report arrived.

Now there is no town that I have been a part of that is more dead on a Sunday afternoon than Washington, DC. The folks in Washington work hard throughout the week, and when the weekend comes, especially staffers who work on the Hill would rather do almost anything than go to the office. However, for the senior staff on the Judiciary Committee, this was not a normal Sunday. We had been waiting for this day. This was why we had prepared the committee and our Republican Conference for the battle that was ahead. The report that the Democrats depended on to take out Donald Trump was now upon us. So, I finished my grocery shopping and got back to the house as quickly as possible.

I did not know what was in the report; I did not know how we would respond. But what I did know was that time was up: the report, at least the attorney general's part, was about to be released. To be honest, after talking with the attorney general and listening to what I thought he would do, I did not expect a summary of the report to be the first thing released. I did expect that he would discuss what the report said about its investigation and the conclusions it found, with maybe some documentation from the report itself. Instead, Bill Barr did something that initially may have seemed to cause frustration and chaos, but I believe was really designed to get the world focused on the priority findings in the report. He focused on the fact that although there was a thorough investigation, the team did not find that Russia and the Trump campaign colluded to win the 2016 election and that there would be no obstruction charges based on the findings of the investigation. The interesting point that came out of this presentation was that Deputy Attorney General Rod Rosenstein concurred with the findings in this report. The Democrats all along had been applauding the work of the deputy, believing that he would be helpful in making the case against President Trump. This was not what the Democrats wanted or anticipated. So in good Washington form, if you do not like what the report says…ATTACK the report and the one who gave it to you.

Now do not think for a minute that this report was of interest only to the folks in the Judiciary Committee. No, I was under direction that the minute we knew what was going on that we were to involve the leadership of our conference. I called Kevin McCarthy, the minority leader, and let him know that the attorney general's response was going to be delivered in the next thirty minutes. He asked if I knew what it would say, and of course, I had to tell him my thoughts are that it would be good for the president, but we would just have to wait and see what was sent over. We decided that we did not want to leave communication about the report up to individual members trying to figure out how best to respond. That meant that we needed to schedule a call that evening to address the whole conference and let them know what we had been given. What was supposed to be a lazy afternoon instead kicked into high gear, and the race was on.

Now, one thing that the attorney general and his team had complete control over was that once they did what was required under law—notifying the chairmen and ranking members of the Judiciary Committee—they were free to do with the information whatever they felt was best and in any manner they saw fit. We had been told this by their office when we had requested that they give us a heads-up on the report before releasing it to a wider audience. We were told that would occur, but we were not told how long we would get, only that they would follow the law and that we would be notified first. When the knock came at the door of our office in Rayburn House Office Building, the room was alive with excitement. Brendan called me and said they were going to scan the document and send it to me. The curve ball that we did not realize was that the attorney general's office was true to their word that we would see it first, but what they did not say is that as soon as the delivery agents finished the deliveries, they would release the document to the world! That meant we were going to have to field questions on the fly and try to make sense of what was said with the public, which was seeing the document at basically the same time. There was no time to waste, and the team kicked into action. We had to get a press statement out and begin to prepare for a Republican Conference that night to let them know the best way to discuss the findings so we could have a unified response to what turned out to be the victory for the president we had all thought it would be.

On the other side of the aisle, however, this was a bitter defeat. They had promised themselves that this would be the tool they needed to rid the nation of Trump. But now they were left at the impeachment altar with nothing to use. Instead of taking the results and dealing with them, they attempted to manipulate the response and, at the same time, begin to tear down the one who gave it: Bill Barr, who instantly became the worst person in America. This respected lawyer who was serving his second time as attorney general, who came back to the job out of an obligation to get the department back on solid footing after the disastrous previous years, was being portrayed as nothing but a small-time hack, who was doing nothing but the president's bidding. The rhetoric was bitter, and the warm, sunny day in March began to turn cold and dark as the Democrats, who felt their opportunity to get rid of the president slipping away, dug in for a fight to turn the narrative around at all costs.

The letter from the attorney general, while answering the questions of findings as it relates to the Mueller report, did not satisfy the media or the Democrats, who had for so long hoped for a definitive negative outcome as it related to the president. The attacks were quick and coordinated. The main thrust being that it did show problems, even collusion and assuredly obstruction. But since the president's attorney general, along with the deputy attorney general, decided that nothing was chargeable, the only logical conclusion was that the special counsel was leaving it to Congress to decide what to do with the information. And most believed that this was the open door for Congress, in this case the House, to open an impeachment investigation into President Trump based on the report's findings.

The problem was the report was not the slam dunk they were expecting. They now would have to attempt to make something out of nothing. The problem was that nothing they had was what they had told the American people all along would be the answer to what they viewed as the corruption of Donald Trump. During the weeks after the release of the letter from Bill Barr, in which he said he would make almost all of the report public, the push became louder and louder from Chairman Nadler and other Democrats: Let us see the full report, and we will make the determination of what it really said. It will be up to us to show that the impeachable offenses were there, just hidden by an accomplice of the president in the Department of Justice, namely the attorney general.

To get a frame of reference for the depth and scope of the Mueller investigation, all you need to do is look at the numbers that define this investigation. According to the reports that were put out during the investigation and summed up in the letter from Bill Barr, the investigation was extremely thorough. It encompassed 40 FBI personnel, over 2,800 subpoenas, nearly 500 search warrants, more than 230 orders for communications records, and over 500 witness interviews. The cost of the Mueller investigation was over $32,000,000! It was apparent enough to us, and to most people who took an objective look at the report, that if these highly skilled and very accomplished attorneys—who had every resource they could want and, as President Trump often reminded the world (and with which I agreed), leaned Democratic in their politics—could not find anything to bring charges on, then maybe we just admit the obvious and say there was nothing there. The idea that they went through this process to simply say it should be left to Congress to interpret the information as a call from the investigators to begin an impeachment inquiry was one of the most amusing and sad commentaries coming out of the release of the report.

After the summary was released, I could see a visible difference in the Democrats on the Judiciary Committee. Chairman Nadler was in denial. He did not want to talk, and when he did, it was with a vitriol that struck me as someone who had seemingly lost his purpose in life. Chairman Nadler had risen to his position based on the argument that he should be the one to take the information from the investigation and lead the impeachment fight in the Judiciary Committee. The committee was at a standstill, and the Democrats were now paralyzed with indecision. We had three months of work in which the most the Democrats could show for it were show hearings, disastrously run markups on highly partisan bills that had no hope of becoming law, and now an albatross of a report that left them with few to no options. They could either embrace the fact that the president did nothing wrong or impeachable, or they could double down and begin to push forward with a series of impeachment-like hearings designed to show that, contrary to what the world could see in the report for themselves, the Democrats knew better and they would prove it.

While Chairman Nadler and the other anti-Trump members of the committee on the Democrats' side plotted what to do, you could sense a shift in the sentiment from many other Democrats. I was beginning to sense the shift in a few of the senior Democrats on the committee who would reach out to us and want to try and get back to working on things like immigration or criminal justice reform. But even they knew that it was not possible as long as the lust for revenge on the president was still firing the emotions of many of their members. I had one conversation with a Democrat more practical than some of his colleagues who lamented the fact that they had gained the majority only to have it given away to the whims of a few who only worried about how to affect the president. It was also becoming very apparent that our strategy of making the majority on the committee work for everything they got and follow the rules was beginning to take a toll on the committee's standing with the leadership and the other members in the Democratic Party. The complete inability of Chairman Nadler to handle the committee without it turning into a side show of yelling and acrimony was beginning to show. We only wanted to use the tools available to us to make our points about legislation and the direction of the committee on certain issues. Instead of the majority being patient and allowing us our time and amendments, they would push and fight and keep things constantly in churn. This made for horrible optics for the committee and its work.

I did not know at the time how bad it was becoming, but we did know that in Speaker Pelosi's office the drumbeat of impeachment was an unwelcome issue. She wanted to portray a majority that was governing and looking out for the American people. Instead she was watching a train wreck of a committee that just happened to be at the very forefront of the impeachment discussion. Democratic staff members would come by and ask me what was going on in the committee; after I explained the problems with leadership and just the basic problems of getting through a hearing or markup, they would just shake their head and mutter out loud about how this was getting out of hand. The problems with the basic mechanics of running a committee would eventually lead to the Speaker's office sending in another person to help them try and navigate the process from a parliamentary perspective. These were just some of the problems the Democrats were having, and to my amazement it was about to get worse.

As the excitement from the release of the Mueller report to the public with the redactions that the attorney general had indicated that he would make continued around Washington, DC, what amazed me the most was the reactions that my Democratic colleagues had to the information that was provided to them. The juvenile way in which they handled the release of the information just heightened the concerns within the rest of the Democrat Conference that the Judiciary Committee may not be the up to the task of investigating the president, much less speaking for the conference on these issues. It appeared that the Democrats were just looking for ways to appear like spoiled kids who did not get their way. When the report was released, they continued the calls for impeachment, adopting the line that it was actually a report for them, and that Mueller left it open for them to now do their work. Messrs. Swalwell, Cicilline, Cohen, and others were a steady sight on the TV, talking about how Bill Barr was a problem and that he mischaracterized the report so that it favored the president. The main problem, however, was that the world could read the report for themselves and see that the report's conclusions were as the attorney general stated.

I said earlier that at first I was not sure that the way the attorney general approached the problem was right. I defended it because the summary was a chance to put the report in context, and we had his promise that the report would be released and that we could all read the details that affected his declarations. After the report was released, it was apparent to me and others that his approach was spot on. It focused the world on the conclusions that came after a thorough reading of the report and not a line-by-line impression that, if taken out of context, could be used to show a different result from the whole.

The Democrats, who never try to let a real or made-up controversy go to waste, took the approach that it was not the whole of the report but the parts that were the real story, and that was where they could make their smoke and mirrors case. The problem was, even with that strategy, you had to have a rational response to reading what was offered by the department regarding the whole of the report, even those parts that had been redacted. The Democrats took the position that if all the report was not redacted then they would not read any of the un-redacted materials and hold out for the whole. This presented a visual and practical problem that they had not thought through. The attorney general agreed to make the redactions available to the leadership of the Judiciary Committees if we would come to the Department of Justice and view them. He had made everything available except the parts that were deemed national security restricted. So, after all the fuss from the Democrats about not getting the entire report, approximately 99 percent of the report was now available for viewing. Yet that was not good enough.

The week that they decided to make the unredacted report available, we were on a district work week. That is, House members were back in their districts, taking meetings and catching up on their work back home. So, it was not the most convenient of times for the release. Nevertheless, after talking to my team, I knew I would have to head back to DC to review the documents. The chairman had made it clear he was not going to view them, but I was not going to pass up the opportunity to get more insight into this investigation. So, with that as the backdrop—the Democrats sticking to an ever more intractable position on their demands of the report's release—I went to see what was offered.

I have often said that most folks do not think the politicians or celebrities they see on television are like them; they do not think they have everyday problems like them. I wish that was true in my case. But at the end of the day, no matter what office I serve in, I am a husband and father, and just a normal middle-aged guy who has problems just like everyone else. If you have ever seen pictures of me, you realize that I wear glasses. I can see to get around without them, but when it comes to reading, I am shut down without my glasses. So, when I woke up that morning and began to get ready, I certainly did not need to have my glasses become a source of problems.

I finished getting dressed and got in the car and started to drive to the airport. When I got to the airport, I was getting out of my car, and in my usual graceful fashion, as I was closing the door my head was in the way, and the door caught my glasses and knocked them off my head. I picked up my glasses, and in the process of opening them to put them on my face, they broke in two pieces. One of the posts in the middle of the glasses between the two lenses came apart. At first, I thought maybe I could put them back together, but the more I tried, the worse they became; they were not going to be fixed by me, and a flight that was leaving soon would not wait.

I had no opportunity that morning to get them fixed. So, I put the pieces in my coat pocket and made my way to the gate. When I got to DC, I explained to the staff what had happened, and after they quit laughing, they realized that I had a real problem. How was I to read the new report without my glasses? After some time, we decided that once I got in the room, I would take out the two parts and use them like monocles. One side would stay on without having to be held, and I would hold the other side in place. At one point as I was reading the report, I forgot I was holding part of the glasses and let go, and it fell on the report. I could do nothing but laugh at the thought that while the media waited and I was in the room with a report that everyone was anxious to see, I was struggling with a pair of broken glasses. It was, in retrospect, appropriate because just like my glasses, which worked only when I could hold them at the right angle, the Democrats were looking at the report with their own broken glasses, trying to make the world believe they were the ones seeing twenty-twenty when they were simply propping up a house of cards.

After reading through the unredacted parts of the report with my staff, I left the building and met with the press who had gathered, waiting to hear if there was any information that was uncovered that changed my feelings or conclusions. I gave the following statement and answered a few questions:

> I do encourage my colleagues, the Democrats, who have asked for transparency, who have asked for access, to actually come here and do just that. Do not come here and take advantage of the attorney general and his offer, to me it says that they're not worried about what's in the report, they're more worried about actually scoring political points.

After I finished the impromptu press conference, I got back in the car, headed to the airport, and went to get my glasses fixed. It was a day that was all about perspective. I went to read what was being offered by the department, while the Democrats led by Chairman Nadler were issuing subpoenas for information they knew they were not allowed to have. This was the heart of the problem: they did not get what they wanted, but they could not let it go. If they relented, the narrative that they had been trying to spin about the president would unravel, and they would be left with nothing. So, they just kept clinging to the thought that the Mueller report was like those little decoder rings that you would get in the Cracker Jack boxes, which was to lead them to act on something even Robert Mueller would not act upon. In the grand scheme of things, my glasses being broken would be an apt analogy of what the Democrats would try next. They wanted to frame their hearings on the Mueller report and a hearing with Bill Barr as impeachment-lite. They knew they could not start a real impeachment trial, so it was up to them to take the out-of-focus and broken view and convince everyone that what they clearly could see was wrong. They had to show that Mueller was only a piece of the puzzle after years of saying it was the whole thing. How do you do that? DISTRACTION and SHOWMANSHIP.

The Democrats knew that, if they were to have any chance of using the report to further their cause, they had to have hearings that would be framed as impeachment hearings but not really. In other words, they changed the rules of the committee, especially in regard to the questioning of people who appeared at these hearings. One of the saddest moments of the day was hearing that the members of the Judiciary Committee on the Democrat side of the aisle did not want to ask questions; they wanted to use the high-powered lawyers that Chairman Nadler had brought in for the purpose of impeachment to ask questions. They wanted this to seem like it was not just a normal hearing but a special hearing with superpowers in order to really show the American people that, regardless of what they read, Mueller was actually saying that the president was guilty and he left it for the committee to finish. It is amazing the arrogance of the chairman and his members to believe that the Mueller team, with an unlimited bank account, unlimited manpower, and subpoena power to compel testimony, was somehow unable to find things but a committee with limited power and limited resources was going to finally find the true story. Only in Washington can that type of stupidity be accepted.

What would unfold over the next couple of months, in May and June 2019, should go down in the annals of the history of the Judiciary Committee as some the worst displays of desperation ever to be brought to the committee room. Chairman Nadler wanted to impose his new scheme of committee rules on a set of hearings that would be used to let the Democratic base know that they had not given up. Although the Mueller report was a complete disaster in terms of helping them try and impeach the president, they were still fighting. If they did not have the substance, they would provide the theatrics that would make the world believe something that was not true. The president had not done anything wrong, and they could not stand it.

First up on the wish list was to get Bill Barr to testify before the committee on the Department of Justice and the Mueller investigation. The Democrats and Chairman Nadler wanted to get the attorney general before the committee so that they could unleash the impeachment-lite model. They would invoke the use of staff counsel to question the attorney general, all to make the hearing more about Donald Trump and impeachment rather than getting to a discussion on the actual report and the findings that were made. The attorney general made it clear that he would come and answer questions but that he would not be part of a political circus. So as the stare-down continued, the May 2, 2019, hearing was coming upon us, and the only question was: Would we have a witness?

In Washington, the one thing that is constant is the never-ending contradictions that you can see in any given week. While the drama between Chairman Nadler and the attorney general was playing out in the House, in the Senate, under the direction of Chairman Lindsay Graham, there was no drama. The Senate scheduled the oversight hearing for May 1, 2019, and the attorney general showed up and testified for over six hours, answering questions from both parties and even taking a second round. Even outside observers felt that the attorney general handled himself well. His direct, no-nonsense answers were refreshing and needed at a time in which most were simply talking past each other in these tense times.

It was just what was needed from my perspective. We had been on the front lines of the side show that was the House Judiciary Committee. My hope was that we could get the attorney general before the House Judiciary Committee and let him answer all the questions that members could come up with. I had no doubt that Bill Barr could stand up to the challenge, and I even believed that he could begin to put us on a right path if given the chance. The problem was the Democrats did not seem to want to Bill Barr to testify. You see, if you do not have a point or a way to show your case is real, then you are very satisfied to keep the illusion going. The Democrats wanted Bill Barr but not enough to remove the show and just let him come and testify. So, after a full day of testimony before the Senate Judiciary Committee, Bill Barr was on deck to be in the House the very next day. The only question was whether the Democrats would remove the barriers and let him come or whether their portrayal of these hearings was more important than the information they could gather. I knew that from my seat, the Democrats were more scared of what Bill Barr would say than they let on, and when push came to shove, they chose to play games instead of getting answers. But then again, that is all we had been doing all year.

May 2, 2019, was the day we had been waiting for since the release of the Mueller report: we would finally get to question Bill Barr, or so we thought. What happened that day is a dark spot on the history of the House and the Judiciary Committee. The day that should have been a day of answers and questions would go down in history as the Chicken Day hearing. Instead of being a time of progress, the Judiciary Committee became a circus, a side show full of clowns and props! As the day opened, we knew that due to what I can only classify as incompetence on the part of the chairman and his advisors, the attorney general of the United States would probably not show up for the hearing. I say again the only people on which to place blame for this result are the chairman and his membership, who wanted to have a show that looked like something that it was not, all with the intent of trying to make the president look bad. The one who was not going to play a part in the Nadler side show was Bill Barr.

The scene was all set, and the players were arriving. The committee room was packed with spectators and media. And members of the committee were arriving to see what would happen, especially since we knew that the attorney general, due to the majority's arrogance, would not be coming. So instead of being able to question the attorney general, the Democrats, led by one of their clowns in chief, Steve Cohen from Tennessee, were determined to make the absent attorney general look bad. Alas, they only managed to show themselves for the desperate clowns they were. It is one thing to say that you believe that a witness is scared or is chicken for not showing up to a committee meeting they are scheduled to testify at, but it is quite another to bring props that are designed to draw attention to yourself. It reminds me of advice I once got that said if you are going to do something out of the norm, you may want to do two things: first, ask why you are doing it and whether it fits what you want to do, and second, ask a friend who will be honest with you what they think. I believe that if Congressman Cohen had tried either part of this advice, he would have probably chosen a different approach that morning. Because somewhere in the recesses of Steve Cohen's thought process, he thought it would be funny to bring not only a toy chicken to the committee room to sit at the witness table, but also a bucket of Kentucky Fried Chicken, which he began to eat and pass around to Democratic members, as if he were serving the buffet line at lunch. His ill-advised behavior removed all doubt about his ignorance.

I have been involved in a lot of things in public office, but I am not sure that I have ever been on the side of something so petty and ridiculous, which accomplished two things the perpetrator had not intended. The first is it showed that the one who looked bad that morning was not the man who had just spent over six hours the day before answering questions in the Senate Judiciary Committee; in fact, Barr was vindicated to many for not showing up to a group who behaved like this. The second thing, and I do not believe Steve Cohen or Chairman Nadler or the members who laughed at the prank thought about, was that they had already gone down the line of making a sham of the committee for the first four months with their heavy-handed tactics and willingness to push nothing but an endless desire to impeach Donald Trump, and this did nothing but solidify that reputation.

This episode and some that were about to follow showed that this committee was not a serious group. Later in the year, when the next big story hit and impeachment was talked about again, the Judiciary Committee, whose jurisdiction is impeachment, would be frozen out of the process until the end because its membership had not done their job and instead believed their job was to be class clowns willing to make a mockery of the system they were hoping to use. I pointed out that morning that the only ones scared were the Democrats and for all the false bravado and chicken stunts aside, Bill Barr was the one who looked like the adult, not the chicken-leg-holding congressman. However, I made one more point that morning. I was mad at them just as much for taking away my right, and my Republican committee members' right, to question the attorney general. We were deprived of our rights because they chose a show over the real work of the committee that we were elected to do. I could understand them fearing the attorney general, especially after they had watched him the day before taking on all questions and coming off very credible. The loss that day was not at the feet of the attorney general; it was the loss of decorum and trust in the eyes of the American public. Depending on what side they fell on, they wanted to hear from the attorney general, and instead we got a side plate of Southern Fried theatrics that in the end left everyone feeling a little sick.

Without the attorney general, without any plan to have Robert Mueller testify, the committee Democrats had a problem: How were they to keep momentum they thought they had with the Mueller report if they had no witnesses? In the short time, they decided to do something that would be sure to put the spotlight back on the circus side of the committee. The next week, although it was their actions that caused the attorney general not to show up to start with, they chose to have a hearing for the purpose of holding him in contempt.

The hearing on the contempt motion against Bill Barr was like a lot of things that year in the Judiciary Committee that should have never happened. This was not a noble exercise by an aggrieved committee in the House of Representatives; this was about a committee that was asking the attorney general of the United States to blatantly break the law and give to the committee information that it was not allowed by law to have. They wanted underlying documents, or investigative work product, specifically 6(e) information, which is grand jury testimony, and they wanted the attorney general to submit to the committee's faux impeachment hearings so that he could answer questions from the Nadler special staff attorneys.

Bill Barr would not consent to break the law for them or submit to their show hearings. And what was his reward for doing what he was supposed to do? He was about to be held in contempt by the House. I can assure you that after six hours of back and forth and a straight party-line vote to find him in contempt, the only ones who should have been held in contempt were the Judiciary Committee and its leadership, who had taken one of the oldest committees in the House, one with an amazing history in the timeline of our country. This is the committee that has been the center of presidential impeachments; it has been the committee that tackled civil rights legislation and plotted the nation's response to the 9/11 attacks and every hot button issue from abortion to gun control, and now it was being driven into the ditch of partisanship and bitterness.

To this day, I do not completely understand the position of the chairman and his committee regarding the attorney general's testimony and their stand over the Mueller report. The simple fact was that they were in a bind and had no real answers. It was at this time that I began to make my way around the floor of the House during votes and talk to Democrats who were not on the Judiciary Committee. What I was hearing was remarkably interesting. The rank-and-file members and especially the new members on their side who were not on the Judiciary Committee could not understand what was going on. Hear me clearly: they were not fans of President Trump, but they knew that the political perception of the country as to how they were handling the fallout from the investigation would backfire on them in the next election cycle if they did not handle it properly. The new members who were in tight districts or districts that President Trump won in 2016 were cautious about what was going on, and the antics of the members of the Judiciary Committee were beginning to wear thin.

One new Democrat asked me if it was as bad as it appeared in our committee. I thought they were asking about the rancor and the long hearings with all the fighting back and forth. I told them that it was bad but that the committee had a history of long, tough debates. The member looked at me and said, "That is not what I am talking about. Is our side really that off message that they would make it look so bad?" They went on to say that the best they could hope for in their district was that Chairman Nadler would not hold no more hearings like the ones we were having because instead of helping they were embarrassing. I said that I agreed but that the desire to get the president was stronger than the desire to see the evidence at face value and that until the Democratic leadership wanted to stop it, things would continue as was.

At first, I thought that this was an isolated sentiment and that it was only the nervousness of a new member. But I began having more discussions on the floor, in the House gym, and in the hallways with members on the Democratic side who shared a similar opinion. At first, I felt sad for the committee, because in my heart, I honestly believe that what goes on in Washington, DC, matters and that the role of the Congress is not trivial or a joke. I tried every day I was there to work on legislation that mattered to people. However, we were now in a time in which the work of the people was secondary to the politics of beating President Trump. With that said, I was bothered by the depths to which our committee had sunk. I wanted it to be better, but it was not headed in that direction at all.

On the other hand, these discussions and my off-the-record discussions with members of the press showed that my strategy and the one that was being employed by the members on our side was working. Every time they tried something, we countered. Every time they tried to overrun us, we would follow the rules and throw it right back at them. It was our relentless determination to force them to have to adapt to us that was winning. And the more we pushed, the more desperate they became. And if there's one thing I've learned in my time on this earth, if your strategy is working, you don't back off; instead, you double down. So if they wanted to stay in the lane of stupid, then we would be there to show the world the depths to which they were willing to plunge.

It was not long before we began the next round of hearings that showed they were desperate and, worse yet, seemingly incompetent to get cooperation from the administration. They wanted to hear from White House Counsel Don McGahn, who had played a large role in the Mueller report. But again, the overzealous and ill-prepared committee could never frame the testimony to allow Mr. McGahn to testify. They wanted him out in the open and with no restrictions. He could not, as they would say, hide behind any privileged response. They wanted him to give testimony that would put the president in a bad light and find something to rejuvenate the idea of impeachment. It was just another tilting at windmills. They had no regard for compromise even when it might have given them what they were looking for. So, they had to turn to other ways to get the message out, and what followed was a series of hearings that bordered on the unnatural. They were so desperate to make these hearings appear to be about impeachment they were willing to use any prop they could to relate back even to a prior impeachment.

The rush to find something to focus the American people on the need for impeachment was getting desperate in the Democratic camp. By the time May and June rolled around, the country was losing interest in the Mueller report. They had been assured by the Democrats that the report would be the answer they needed and that Donald Trump would be impeached. Instead, the Democrats were left scrambling, with no plan and no witnesses. And the one witness they could have gotten, Attorney General Bill Barr, they wasted. There is an old saying among lawyers that if in your case, you have the law on your side, you argue the law. If you do not have the law on your side, you argue the facts of your case. And if you have neither the law nor the facts on your side, you simply yell and beat on the table to distract from the fact that you have no case. This latter scenario summed up the situation the Democrats found themselves in.

So, to keep the story going, they had to start having hearings with people who would affirm their version of the Mueller report and talk about how the Justice Department and, specifically, Bill Barr mishandled the investigation. Let us be clear: nothing new was going to come out of these hearings. It was merely another chance to attack the president and say the word impeachment as many times as they possibly could. If they could make the people believe that they were really carrying on an impeachment investigation, then maybe the people would stay with them until they could finally get the hearing they wanted to have—and that was with the man who wrote the report, Robert Mueller. However, since they were never able to get a time set up for Mr. Mueller to come, we began to believe that they really did not want him to come. The report was not what they needed, and they did not want him to merely reinforce the fact that the president had done nothing wrong.

So back to the show hearings, which were designed to keep the focus on the Mueller report and the perceived wrongdoing in the White House. Chairman Nadler started the ball rolling by announcing a "series of hearings" related to special counsel Robert Mueller's Russia report, beginning with a June 10 hearing featuring President Richard Nixon's former White House counsel, John Dean. The hearing was titled: "Lessons from the Mueller Report: Presidential Obstruction and Other Crimes." Its subtitle should have been: We got nothing else, so let's resurrect a figure from the past who has spent the last forty years of his life calling for every president since Jimmy Carter to be impeached over some wrong. The Democrats were digging out the disco records and the bell bottoms. The next big witness on the block would be straight out of the Nixon impeachment, John Dean. The John Dean hearing was an amazing reach, even for the Democrats on the committee, who had been grasping at straws the entire year. The chairman, in a moment of irony, said that the hearing was going to focus on obstruction. I guess the one thing I could agree with was that John Dean had showed himself to be an expert in that field.

However, I also saw him as an expert in another field. It was John Dean who was part of the last big use of the federal government to interfere in an election for president. He had been a part of the last cabal that sought and did use resources of the federal government for nefarious purposes in an election.

On the Republican side, we were happy for any reason that the majority would give us to talk about the corruption that we believed existed at the Obama Justice Department, especially when it involved the investigation into the Trump campaign and its abuse of private citizens' rights in trying to keep Donald Trump from becoming president. The light needed to be shone once again on the likes of Jim Comey, Peter Strzok, Andy McCabe, Jim Clapper, and John Brennan. These who had been so deeply involved in the Operation Crossfire Hurricane investigation could have taken their cues from the one I dubbed the godfather of the illegal use of government resources against private citizens to influence an election. The fact that the Justice Department had members trying to interfere in a presidential election and then—as we found out later—to hinder the new administration in its early formation should concern every American regardless of their political affiliation. As the Republican leader of the committee, I felt it was my job to let the American people know that if there was a connection to the Nixon impeachment it was the use of governmental resources to harass a presidential candidate.

The real purpose of these hearings was to continue to try and build a case with the American people that impeachment was the only avenue that could right the perceived wrongs of Donald Trump. Also, Chairman Nadler knew that one of the restrictions that Speaker Nancy Pelosi had placed on moving forward with an impeachment was that the public had to be on their side. That was not true at this point. So, to increase support, they turned to show hearings. And we just turned on the popcorn machine and went after them at every turn. To convince the public that they were right, they needed to find witnesses who were credible. Instead, the listing of John Dean, a CNN contributor, to come aboard as the first witness was not a show of strength but of desperation. And his testimony bore that out.

The hearing proved to be just what we knew it would be, a pathetic attempt to get headlines to support a failed interpretation of the Mueller report. They believed somehow that if they could just have enough hearings, the words of the Mueller report would either somehow change or, hopefully, from their perspective, begin to move public opinion to their side. Neither of these things happened, and at the end of the day, the hearing was a one-day headline that left John Dean bruised and the rest of their witnesses sounding like desperate commentators begging for someone to believe their version of what Mueller really meant. It is still hard to believe after some time has passed to look back on the desperate attempts made by these witnesses and the Democrats to make people believe that the Mueller report was the great bombshell that should take down President Trump. The truth turned out to be something else, and most Americans seemed to accept the report at face value and saw no need to go forward with impeachment. In fact, off the record, even the press who thought as the Democrats did that the Mueller report would give them the impeachment story they craved began to sense the futility of the Democrats' attempts to repaint the narrative.

The one thing that I did find amusing as I had to sit in my chair on the dais for so many hours listening to the other side drone on was that someone on their side, maybe a staffer or Chairman Nadler, decided that the reason the American people were not ready to impeach the president was not that the report was insufficient but that the American public had not read it. This led to the decision to have a national story time for the American public and by gosh if they won't read it, we will just have to read it for them. And that is just what they did. In hearing after hearing, they would each take time to read passages into the record. Although we had already had it submitted to the record of the committee, they felt like dramatic readings were the trick. So, starting with Chairman Nadler and continuing on down the line, members of the Democratic Party would read passages of the report and then try and ask the called witnesses to comment on the report. It was a painful exercise. Some of the Democrats seemed to have practiced their reading, and some even added their own dramatic interpretation. At one point, I thought David Cicilline was auditioning for a part in a future movie on the subject because when it was his time to read, he would change his voice tone and add emotional inflection to the reading.

Still, at the end of the day, the conclusion never changed: there was no collusion nor any incidents of obstruction that met the standard for charges to be sought against the president. The show droned on, and the Democrats were desperate. The chairman and his staff knew that even though they felt like they had all they needed for their impeachment moment, the Democratic leadership was not convinced. They needed their big break. That option would become the final act of what most of believed their push for impeachment. The time had arrived, even if it was a risk. They had to bring Robert Mueller to the witness table and take one final shot at swaying the American people.

CHAPTER 3:
THE MUELLER TESTIMONY

Stories take many forms, and depending on one's perspective, they can contain different things to those looking at what is seemingly the same incident or situation. Reflecting on the Democrats' obsession with trying to defeat Donald Trump, from the moment of his election to the start of his time as president to the eventual undertaking of the impeachment process, nothing held as constant as their narrative that Donald Trump was corrupt and that he had colluded with the Russians. They never changed their narrative; they clung to it as one would hold to a water bottle in the desert with the sun broiling down. The narrative only got stronger when they felt there was a way to prove all of what they felt or even made up. That way was an investigation by Robert Mueller into the claims of Russian interference into the 2016 election and was extended to investigate claims of obstruction by the Trump administration. The investigation was the Holy Grail for the Democrats and all in the media who wanted to see the administration held accountable for all the wrongs it had supposedly committed. Members on both sides of the aisle would clamor to a microphone to say the special counsel's investigation must be protected. Now remember nothing had appeared or had been presented to the American people that showed any of these bad things were true, but there was a steadfast belief that if Robert Mueller were on the case, then it would find all that is wrong and begin to right the wrong of Donald Trump being elected president.

As I described earlier, when the Mueller report was delivered to the attorney general, he had a choice to make. He decided to do something that no one expected: release a summary that focused on the main points without all the distractions and came to the conclusions that the report gave. This caused people to see the results, and when the report was released, they could see the evidence backing up his summary. Of course, the Democrats did not like this because they wanted to spin it and control the narrative, no matter what the report said. I can still remember trying to talk with Chairman Nadler after the release of the summary, and he was so mad he could not even really talk about it. He just knew the narrative was dying, and he had to scramble to fix it. This was why we had the hearings that did nothing except try and keep the narrative going that the report was really damning even when it was not.

Surprisingly, a few days after the summary was released, Bill Barr got a letter from the special counsel. In his letter he said that the attorney general had caused confusion in his letter and that he should have released his summaries if he was going to release anything. It was the oxygen that Nadler needed to keep the flame going. Nadler and the Democrats began to spin that Mueller was upset and that the summary was wrong. They hammered Bill Barr for supposedly trying to protect the president. The reality was that after the full report was released, it became apparent to an objective viewer that the summary did reflect the outcomes of the report. It was also apparent to many of us that the letter reflected the unhappiness of the partisans on the investigations that their work they had hoped would be damning to the president was not having its intended effect.

It was after this letter and then after the full report was released that I and others began to call for Mueller to testify before our committee to give his account of the report. I was criticized by some for this action, and at times, even the administration was not sure they wanted to have Robert Mueller testify. I, however, felt that the only thing that would put this to rest was to hear from Mueller directly and allow us to question the report. More importantly, it would allow us to question things that the special counsel office did not address like how the whole thing got started to begin with. Why was the cabal at the Department of Justice allowed to coordinate with the intelligence community to open an investigation on a candidate for president and then continue to harass the new administration as they were getting settled into the term? The only way we'd have the opportunity to ask these questions was to have him testify. It was a risk, yes. But being able to ask questions about what they did not investigate would show that this report was not interested in the complete story, only one that focused on the president. It was not concerned about the fact the whole reason they existed was the abuse of the system by those in the Department of Justice who did not like President Trump.

The reality of Mueller testifying was also concerning to the Democrats. They knew that the report was not good for them, and if the hearing was not good, it would be better just to deal with the inanimate report than the author of that report contradicting their spin. It was after the report was released and the chairman was beginning his own sham investigations with fake hearings and demanding folks like Hope Hicks, Don McGahn, and any other person who was mentioned in the Mueller report come to testify that I decided that if they wanted to hear from everyone else about the report but were not trying to get the author, I would use every opportunity to remind the chairman of his mistake. The thing that I realized from traveling across my home state of Georgia and the rest of the country was that people always want to hear from the source, and if they do not get that chance, it leaves doubt in their mind. So, every time I would remind the chairman that they wanted to talk to everyone but Mueller, you could sense the Democrats' palpable concern. Do we get him here to testify? And if we do, how can we make sure that it goes our way? They could not answer those questions, but the pressure was building.

Then on May 29, 2019, Robert Mueller held a press conference announcing the closing of the Office of the Special Counsel and his return to private practice. I do not know how it works out with most people, but with me, it seems that if there is a hard way to go about it, I will find it. When Robert Mueller decided to give this press conference, there was truly little heads-up given to us. The day before, Brendan, my staff director, called and told me that Mueller was giving a press conference and that I needed to watch it. Well, that was going to be difficult along the US border out from El Paso where I was traveling at the time, but we set out to find a way. The only solution was for us to find a high point where I could get cell service and have my office call me. Then I would listen to the conference on my phone. I have to say, having a front seat to history can take you to a lot of places, but little did I expect it would cause me to have to listen to a press conference in the middle of the desert, and not just any press conference. It was Robert Mueller, and there was no telling what he was going to say.

As I listened as best I could, it was obvious that he was not happy with the spin that had surrounded the report and that he wished things had come out better but that he was not upset with the attorney general. He also stated that he reiterated what was in the report, that they operated off the Office of Legal Counsel opinion that you could not charge a sitting president. That one statement alone would give the Democrats talking points to spin for days. The interesting thing was that even if that were the case—which was the opinion of many of us—the investigation did not find anything to charge to start with. So, in the end, this was just a semantics game. The really interesting part of his press conference, however, was his comments about his future and the desire not to discuss this anymore. He stated:

> Now I hope and expect this to be the only time that I will speak to you in this manner. I am making that decision myself. No one has told me whether I can or should testify or speak further about this matter. There has been discussion about an appearance before Congress. Any testimony from this office would not go beyond our report. It contains our findings and analysis and the reasons for the decisions we made. We chose those words carefully and the work speaks for itself. And the report is my testimony. I would not provide information beyond that which is already public in any appearance before Congress.

I may have been in the middle of the desert, but I could have sworn I heard Chairman Nadler and the rest of the Democrats heart hit the floor. By this time, they knew that if they were to ever change

Speaker Pelosi's mind or, even more important, the American people's mind, they had to have Robert Mueller come and testify and not only share the report but tell the world that the Democrats were right. Now he was going to ride off into the proverbial sunset and wash his hands of the whole thing.

I publicly wished him well as he returned to private life, but I also was a little mad. He had an obligation, I believed, to come and defend his report. The report that bore his name was being used to attack a president who had done nothing wrong, and to simply cut and run did not live up to the fabled legacy of Robert Mueller. However, if that was the way he was going to play it, fine. We knew that, in the end, the Democrats needed him more than we did, and if this finally put impeachment as a real option off the table, then good riddance. What we did not realize was this would be the time that Chairman Nadler and his team began real negotiations with a witness to get him to come in. It was a high-stakes move, but if they had any chance, they had to play the card. The negotiations, we learned through staff outreach, was back and forth. One point it appeared to be on, then it would be off. The clock was also ticking because Congress would be gone for August break in a few short weeks, and after five weeks of not being in DC, the momentum for the investigation would be all but dead. Then, finally, the news came that Robert Mueller would testify. It was first scheduled for July 17, 2019, at which time he would testify for two hours before both the House Judiciary Committee and the House Select Committee on Intelligence. Then after more negotiations and complaints that the time was too short, it was rescheduled for July 24, 2019, for three hours. It would still be before both committees, but with three hours it meant that all my members would get to ask a round of questions. The Democrats were not going to get to since they had more members and time would not allow it.

On the morning of July 24, 2019, I woke up and left my office. Yes, I am one of those members who sleeps in my office. I had a side room that was closed off from the rest of the office, and in it was my private area and bathroom. I would typically get up by 5:00 a.m. and would be in the gym by 5:30 or 5:45 a.m. I would go for a run, work out with weights, and then get showered for the day. This morning was one that had a little something special in the air. As I walked down what were normally empty hallways, I ran into media crews who were there early, bringing in the equipment that would be needed to cover the day's events. I found that, unlike me, most of Washington is not a morning crew, especially not the reporters. I remember having pen and pad sessions with the media and scheduling them for 8:30 a.m. It was fun watching these half-awake reporters come in and pretend they were always up and going at this time. The coffee helped, but you could tell they did not want to be there that early. Today was no exception. As I later went to the committee hearing room, I took my normal trek from my office. I had learned that if I came in the main doors of the Rayburn House Office Building, where the committee hearing room was located, I would have to walk about one hundred yards down a hallway, with reporters all lining the halls asking questions. So, I began taking the underground passage and coming up the elevators down from the hearing room and away from the line of reporters. Today, though, it did not matter. They were everywhere, and some of the networks had even sent some of their anchor talent to cover the hearing close up. Today was the day people had been waiting on, and the show must go on.

Walking into the hearing room that day was like what you would expect at something like a national convention. The room was packed! Reporters, staff, cameras, members, and onlookers crowded not only the hearing room but also every hallway leading to the hearing room. As the hour approached for the hearing, a big smile came across my face, and it had nothing to do with the scene in the room that day. No, I knew our team was ready because our members and their staff knew what we needed to do because just like for every big game the team had practiced and we knew what we had to do.

The night before, we decided to stage a mock hearing so that everyone would feel a little more comfortable going into what would be for many of us up to this point one of the biggest hearings we had been a part of. We also had to deal with the problem of time. Even though we had managed to get the time extended to three hours total, it would still be a push to get everybody on our side to ask their round of questions.

This was important to me because all our members had endured so much from the year already. Chairman Nadler had made life miserable during most markups and hearings. It was our time to get our questions in for Robert Mueller, and we had to be ready. Now I was not sure how this was going to go. In Congress, it is not like you can withhold a scholarship if someone will not participate with the team, but I was so happy to see that everyone showed up for the mock hearing. We set up in one of the other judiciary hearing rooms and in the same order as we would be for the real thing. I had our lead investigator, Carlton Davis, prepare as Robert Mueller. Carlton had been through hearings with Mueller before, and he did a great job perfecting the old Robert Mueller: the Mueller attitude and answering style. It gave the members a very realistic look at what they might expect the next day. I was amazed at how much preparation everyone had put into their questions. One of the main goals of the hearing was for us to cover as much ground as we could. We knew this would be our only time to question Mueller, and we needed to make it count. The Democrats wanted to make this about impeaching the president. We wanted to make it about Mueller and the predicate for the investigation to start with, which we knew they had ignored. We wanted the American people to see that we were not just sitting back and accepting whatever they were trying to sell, but rather that we were pushing back with the truth.

I am often asked what it is about Congress that is good because there are plenty of things that make it exceedingly difficult to serve in. I can tell you that nights like this are what makes Congress special and a place most will never understand. In the room that night we had amazing leaders like Jim Sensenbrenner and Steve Chabot, who had been through the wars and were still in there helping others. The example of the older members was invaluable for the freshman and sophomore members preparing for their first big hearing. I was amazed at how on our side the members took seriously their practice. Everyone saw the passion of Jim Jordan and Louie Gohmert and Matt Gaetz in the live hearing, but I am here to tell you they practiced like the played. We even had to calm Louie down because Carlton played Mueller so well that Louie was getting mad at what he knew would be Mueller's answers. That is what made this simulation effective. The new members had a chance to ask and perfect their questions in the safety of the group and left with a better perspective on what would work and what would not. That kind of feedback was invaluable and would prove highly effective later in the year when we were back at it. I left the room that night knowing we were ready.

Relationships are the most important currency in the world, but in Congress they are the thing that makes the high-pressure world bearable. It also did my heart good to know that while we were practicing substantive questions the Democrats had been practicing as well but they were working on how they would respond to us using procedural motions to disrupt the hearing. It was good to find out they become aware of what I told our team at the first meeting, which was I wanted them to always have what we were going to do in the back of their mind. It was good to live rent free in their heads. It also became very apparent that they did not need much practice except for reading because instead of letting their members come up with their questions, they scripted their entire set and printed it off. If I had wanted to, I could have tweeted the next set of questions coming from the Democrats because Chairman Nadler had the script, and as he called on each of his members, he would follow along on the script making sure that each of his members read what they were supposed to. I guess they were so scared they would get it wrong they had to give them the script to keep them on track. In the end, as the memory of the night before faded, the noise of the room came streaming back, and I knew we were ready. It was show time.

The room was electric that morning. You could just sense that history would hold this day in remembrance; for some, especially the Democrats, thought this was victory day. After Robert Mueller testifies, they thought they would be vindicated, and the world would see that what they have been saying about Donald Trump was right all along. On our side we just wanted to finally be able to ask questions to the man who ran an investigation we believed was started on a false narrative and was designed for one thing and one thing only: find things that could be used against Donald Trump and hide what appeared to be wrongdoing at the Department of Justice and in other agencies in the Obama administration when it came to spying on political enemies.

As the chairman gaveled the hearing to order, I could tell he was more nervous than for most hearings. I believe that he knew this was a pivotal moment for not only the strategy that he had led the committee down in its obsession with the president, but also for him personally and his leadership style. Chairman Nadler was becoming more and more agitated that the world did not see things like he and his committee members did. Robert Mueller would hopefully provide a breath of fresh air for his efforts that he could use to convince the Democratic leadership that this was a winnable pursuit. As he started his opening statement you could hear in his voice the stress of the day. He had invested so much into the moment that each word seemed to pour out with an urgency that screamed for validation.

For my part I was glad this day was here. I was not expecting anything new to come out of the hearing, but you never truly know what will happen until the questions start flying and the answers are given. Chairman Nadler started it off and went a little long but that was not uncommon, and his line of questions tried to paint the narrative that Donald Trump was guilty of the things he was accused of—namely, collusion and obstruction—but the special counsel was unable to finish his job because the Department of Justice policy of not indicting a sitting president prohibited him from charging this president. In his questioning you could sense the desperation and nervousness in Nadler's voice. When he finally yielded time to me, I knew that the first thing that I needed to do was to frame the hearing in its proper context, and that would lay the groundwork for the rest of our side to question the many aspects of the investigation while allowing the report to stand on its own as one that had failed to make a case against the president.

My team and I had worked out a plan that would hopefully box Mueller into his own words, thus limiting what may or may not come out over the next few hours. I began to bring out the fact that in his press conference he stated that he really had nothing to say about the report and that it stood on its own. As he said, it speaks for itself. This may seem simple, but it was important to us that we were only dealing with testimony that was in the report and not anything new or outside what was already reported. We did not want him to use this time to talk about things that were not in the report that we would not have been able to examine and would be asked to take his word for. No, we wanted him to be true to his word and only discuss his conclusions as they were laid out in the report. No late editorial statements that would be used by the Democrats to continue their own folly of investigation. After going down a rather long list of deposition-style questions in which I contained myself to go slow in my speaking style, we stumbled on to an exchange that set the tone for the rest of the hearing and revealed that this was not going to be the old Robert Mueller. He was older and tired, and it showed. He really did not want to be there, but what was more disturbing was he did not have a good grasp on the facts in the report, which for us just confirmed that much of this work was handled by those who were not fans of the president. The Robert Mueller of old would have swatted questions away and shown a firm grasp of the facts, but this Robert Mueller was a shadow of his old self, as his testimony would show.

As I came to the end of my questions, I asked about collusion and conspiracy. This was important because the Democrats and the press were always saying that the president was guilty of collusion with the Russians. The problem with that is there is no federal crime of collusion. Conspiracy, however, is different story, in that it very much is a defined federal crime. The casual nature in the way the Democrat and many in the media implied that these terms were one in the same was used to bolster the claims of wrongdoing by President Trump. In our reading of the report, we found something that I wanted to bring out. The report writers stated that collusion and conspiracy were commonly thought of as the same but in the context of this investigation the president had done nothing with the Russians that was wrong no matter whether you called it collusion or conspiracy. This was important to note because some had taken to saying of course he had not colluded, what he really had done was conspire with the Russians. In other words, semantics may matter, but in this case, we will use the words how we want for the intended effect of getting the president. So, when I asked a simple question of the special counsel—"Did you believe that in everyday or colloquial thought the words *collusion* and *conspiracy* have the same meaning?"—his answer set off what would be a break from the old Mueller, and the new Mueller would be on display the rest of the day. He replied that no, they were not the same. In planning for this question, we planned for two contingencies. The first was that he stuck with the report and answered yes, they are thought of the same but really are not. The next was that he answered no, and I would immediately be able to impeach his testimony with his own words from the report. So, when he said no, I immediately called up the quote in the report page 180 volume one that read:

> As an initial matter, this Office evaluated potentially criminal conduct that involved the collective action of multiple individuals not under the rubric of "collusion," but through the lens of conspiracy law. In so doing, the Office recognized that the word "collude[e]" appears in the acting attorney general's August 2, 2017, memorandum; it has frequently been invoked in public reporting; and it is sometimes referenced in antitrust law, see, e.g., Brooke Group v. Brown & Williamson Tobacco Corp., 509 U.S. 209, 227 (1993). But collusion is not a specific offense or theory of liability found in the U.S. Code; nor is it a term of art in federal criminal law. *To the contrary, even as defined in legal dictionaries, collusion is largely synonymous with conspiracy as that crime is set forth in the general federal conspiracy statute*, 18 U.S.C. § 371.

It was at this point we saw what would become a pattern for the rest of the day. What should have been a simple question and answer became elusive. He would refer to the report and then he would change his answer. It was in that moment that I knew this day was not going to go as the Democrats had hoped; in fact, I believed that it would finally put to rest the use of the Mueller report as a tool to impeach the president. If the Democrats wanted to use the report, they would have to convince the American people that the performance they saw today was enough to trust when it came to judging with confidence the results of the report. As he said in his opening statement, the report is his testimony. We now had him confined to the report, and anything outside the report would be suspect, as he had already stated they had no new evidence and anything offered would be for propping up or trying to expand something that they had already admitted was closed. The hearing parameters were set, and we now could execute knowing that the hearing would be about what we knew, the report, and not extra evidence brought up to help improve the report from the Democrats' perspective. Robert Mueller was only ten minutes into questions, and he already looked tired. It was going to be a long day for him.

We had one more element to our game plan, and that was to be executed by John Ratcliffe, who later would become the director of National Intelligence. John is a former United States attorney and had worked with Robert Mueller during his time in the Justice Department. He is also known as an through and skilled questioner on our committee. His job was to show the report to be out of step not only with the practices of the Justice Department but against the very notion that in this country a person is innocent until proven guilty. The Mueller report contained a sentence that Democrats used to the detriment of the president: "[W}hile this report does not conclude that the president committed a crime, it also does not exonerate him." Congressman Ratcliffe made a point that this type of statement was not the job of a prosecutor. The prosecutor, in this case the special counsel, was to decide whether anything was chargeable and if so to charge it, or find that it was not and leave it alone. We believed that this line about exoneration had been left in the report because the attorneys on the case knew they could not make the case against the president but wanted to leave doubt in the minds of people who read the report. This type of prosecutorial cowardness was unacceptable, and as Ratcliffe made this point you could see the façade of Robert Mueller's strength begin to slip away. In my mind this report, written by his associates, left a stain on Mueller's reputation, which up until then had been unimpeachable.

We knew that they public would turn away quickly since most of these hearings turn boring quickly, so we knew we had to hit our best shots up front. After our first lines of questioning, we did just that. It was said that thirteen million folks tuned in to see the hearing and after the first fifteen minutes of questioning the story line was set. Robert Mueller looked weak and unorganized, and the information coming out was not new. In fact, for all the Democrats' desire to make the report dispositive against the president, the American people saw the obsession by the Democrats on full display, not only in our Judiciary Committee hearing, but also during the Intel Committee hearing that followed. When it was all over, no one who honestly assessed the report and Mueller's performance no longer thought it held the cards for impeachment.

The determination that the day was a disaster for not only the Democrats but also Robert Mueller was not just the Republican perspective. Across the board the media that had seemingly so hoped that Robert Mueller would deliver a blow to the president came away shaken and frustrated.

The Democrats played the only card they had, and it was a dud. The hearing was not a magic bullet for the Democrats. In fact, every time they thought they could walk Robert Mueller up to saying that they were right, he would chop down their arguments with a subtle "I do not agree with that assessment." The worst problem, however, was not the Democrats and their repeated attempts to prove the case against Donald Trump, which did not exist; it was the showing of Robert Mueller himself. He had once been a man whose impeccable reputation preceded him; now, he was just a man who looked out of sorts, bored, and not in command of the facts and the room, which we had all come to expect from him. It also reinforced to many of us that this was not coming from Mueller but rather the gaggle of partisans who had been hired to run the investigation. I believe they thought that under the cover of the Mueller name they could do whatever they wanted, and no one would question it. The reality is that when you use someone else's name and reputation, your own actions have to match the one you are using. In this case the lawyers seemed to get caught up in their pursuit and let the desire of the moment to find something wrong bring down not just them but the man that they claimed to admire, Robert Mueller.

The reviews of the hearing came in swift and hard. Democrat David Axelrod tweeted: "This is very, very painful." MSNBC's Jeremy Bash was quoted as saying, "I have to say that far from breathing life into the report, he kind of sucked the life out of the report. I thought he was boring. I thought in some cases he was sort of evasive, he did not want to explain or expand on his rational. He seemed lost at times. He was flipping through the report, trying to find passages that members of Congress were reading to him. I thought it slowed things down. And I thought it really was a very ineffective defense of his own work."

* * * * *

With the Mueller report and Robert Mueller's testimony behind us, we had lived through seven months of Democrat obsession with Donald Trump. My hopes were that going into the August break we would all be able to put this behind us and recognize that President Trump had done nothing wrong and was not leaving office so let's try and accomplish something for the American people. The border was still on fire, and other issues like criminal justice reform and intellectual property, which had been left on the sidelines while the majority chased their obsession with Donald Trump, could now again be brought up and dealt with. The problem for the Democrats, however, was that we were headed into the presidential election cycle, and as they surveyed the political landscape they realized they probably were not going to beat President Trump. So, they had to continue to try and find a way to tear him down.

We left Washington for what we all hoped would be a time of rest and recharging so that when we come back, we could maybe get something done. At least that was the hope. Little did we know that the day after the Mueller hearing, less than twenty-four hours later, the foundation for the next big push by the Democrats to impeach Donald Trump would happen. While we were enjoying the fact that we felt we had finally put to rest the Mueller report, the president made a phone call to the president of Ukraine to congratulate him on his victory. Little did anyone know, but also listening in on the call was someone who took offense at what they thought the president's intentions were on the call, and with that the flame that was impeachment, which the world thought had died on the floor of the Judiciary Committee hearing room, was a few short weeks from blazing into a formal impeachment process. The problem for the Democrats was that the clock and the calendar were now an even more demanding tyrant.

CHAPTER 4:
RECESS

Sometimes in life you can tell exactly what is happening and what is next. Sometimes you have no idea, and that would be the fall of 2019. As the month of July ended, we finished our work in the House and departed for what I thought would be a good month back at home getting caught up on all the things that had piled up due to what had been going on with the committee and the new life under Democratic control in the House. I felt a sense of pride as I left Washington and headed home for the break.

We, on the committee, had become a battle-tested group in which both members of the committee and staff performed at a high level under difficult circumstances. Books are often written about what the members do in Washington, DC. Being a member, I am aware of all that we go through and the work that it entails, but if we did not have our staffs, who put in long hours and give us perspective into our jobs that is invaluable, nothing would get done. The minority staff on the Judiciary Committee had performed in an amazing manner. Led by Brendon Belair, the staff director; Bobby Parmiter, a veteran of the committee from the majority days; Jon Ferro, who was so powerful as our parliamentarian; Erica Barker; Ella Yates; Jessica Andrews; and Amanda Thompson. These folks, along with the members personal staff, had pulled together and were amazing. Almost all of these great staffers were under thirty years of age. I am often asked about my feelings about the future of our country. I can safely say that if these great folks are indicators of what lies ahead, then this country is in great hands. However, the one thing I knew was they were tired, and it was time for them to put aside the eighty-hour weeks and get some time off. My hope was that when the members got out of town, they would be able to get some rest and recharge the batteries, because the one thing I knew was that the Democrats were not going to let up. We may have derailed their hopes for the Mueller report and the rest of the agenda that year, but they would come back in September, and we would be at it again.

As the break began, we were not able to stay quiet for long. On August 3, 2019, a mentally ill man walked into a Walmart in El Paso, Texas, and proceeded to kill twenty-three people and injure twenty-three more, setting off a firestorm of debate and proposals about guns and violence in our country. There was talk about the chairman calling us back in early to take up gun control legislation. We knew that it would not go anywhere, but we still had to be prepared for whatever the chairman wanted to do. The only new wrinkle in the scenario was that the White House was seeing if there was any gun safety legislation that they could get behind.

Normally in August, I try and catch up with some of my active-duty training in the United States Air Force. I have been in the Air Force Reserve since 2002 and even served in Iraq in 2008. I decided to stay active in the Air Force even with my hectic schedule in Congress. So, while I was back on my base in Warner Robins, Georgia, I headed back to the hotel each evening to talk with the administration about how to deal with the Democrats' renewed push for gun control considering the tragedy in El Paso. At the end of it all, the discussions never progressed past what had already passed earlier in the House. The Senate was still in Republican control and had no interest in taking up this legislation. When we got back in September most members envisioned that we would be dealing with the spending deadline of September 30 to keep the federal government going.

All in all, a relatively quiet August was taking shape, but little did we know that July 25 call was floating around not only the executive branch but also it was in the hands of Congressman Adam Schiff and his committee staff. On August 12, 2019, a third-party whistleblower filed a complaint accusing the president of acting inappropriately on the call. What we only found out later was this person was just the start of what many Democrats would come to believe was another opportunity to remove Donald Trump from office. Adam Schiff was now in control, and he had no intention of letting this opportunity go to waste.

Now what transpired over the next four months in the House can only be described as surreal. By this time, I had been in Congress for almost seven years. I had been there for the shutdown of 2013. Little did I know then that shutting down the federal government would become an event almost as regular as the cherry blossoms each spring. I have witnessed a Speaker resign and a new Speaker reluctantly take the chair. I had seen the dysfunction that is Congress up close and personal. I can say that most days in the modern Congress, you could look up *chaos theory* in the dictionary, and it would cite Congress as an example. But as with chaos theory, something that seems completely random does have its own sense of order. It is that theory that the rest of 2019 would play out with the Democrats clinging to the faintest of hopes they could get rid of Donald Trump by spinning a fantastic narrative of suspicion, rule-bending, and doubt while at the same time trying to hide the reality that the chaos they were promoting was actually a well-designed plan to finally tag President Donald Trump with the label of being impeached.

Now before we begin the descent into the valley, it is worth taking a quick look at our country's history with impeachment. Before this Congress, there were a few things that every person, no matter their ideology, could agree to. The first would be that although the Founders seemed to believe that impeachment might be used often, it has turned out not to be the case. In fact, before this episode there were only two other times a president was impeached, President Andrew Johnson in 1868 and President Bill Clinton in 1998. The House of Representatives began an impeachment process against then President Richard Nixon but was never acted upon since President Nixon resigned before the articles could be formally voted on by the House as a whole. It also is undisputed that the impeachment inquiries for these individuals were not rushed agendas but rather investigations that spanned long periods and fully engaged all parties that were involved. It is a fact that by the time the impeachment inquiries were opened in the House, especially for both Mr. Nixon and Mr. Clinton, the facts of the cases were agreed to by both sides, which only left the political question of whether Congress would proceed with the hearings to decide if impeachment was the proper course to take given the evidence set forth.

It should also be noted that although in every impeachment before this one involving President Trump involved a known crime being violated, it is not required for impeachment. Inherently, Congress can impeach a president for almost any reason if it has the votes and is willing to endure the political fallout from its actions. Despite risky odds and no case for impeachment, the Democrats, who I contend not only wanted to get this president but also to ensure that they did political damage, were willing to assume any risk political or otherwise to move forward to keep a promise they had made to the liberal base in the party: we will hold President Trump accountable, and we will get rid of him. The problem is that when you are driven by outside sources such as time and political pressure you will cut corners and do whatever you have to do to make it happen. The Democrats, this time led by Adam Schiff, would have no problem doing just that. Thus the fall was going to be a constant fight to take the contents of a phone call and make it into something that I believe even they did not think was enough.

PART TWO:

THE PHONE CALL BETWEEN PRESIDENT TRUMP AND UKRAINIAN PRESIDENT ZELENSKY

CHAPTER 5:
THE SCHIFF SHOW

When we arrived back in Washington after the September break, no one knew what was going to happen. All through the month of August, Brendan and Bobby on my staff would reach out to Chairman Nadler's staff to see what kind of agenda they wanted to pursue when we got back. Remember, no one at this time except for members of the executive branch and (as we came to find out later) Adam Schiff and his committee staff knew anything about the call or much less the whistleblower's report on the call. So we came back with no idea what Chairman Nadler was wanting to focus on with the committee especially after the Mueller hearing had left such a bitter taste in the Democrats' mouths. He had placed all he had in a bet on Robert Mueller and his investigation, and it had been a bust. In the process he had turned the Judiciary Committee into a place in which the rules of the committee and the House were abused and broken so much that even members who were not on the Judiciary Committee were talking about it. I can remember a Democrat who came up to me one morning earlier in the year after one of our more unhinged hearings and asked, "What in the hell is going on in your Committee? It looks like a circus, and it is making us all looks bad." This Democrat was expressing what many on their side felt. They did not like President Trump and were hoping against all hope they could beat him in the next election, but they did not see what was happening in the committee as particularly helpful. They understood that fairness was what they controlled, and they did not want to give the appearance that they were so obsessed with Donald

Trump that they could not do anything else. It was not an uncommon complaint to hear from some in the Democrat Conference that the constant hearings and the side show that they had become were hurting the members who did not even sit on the committee. They wanted to be tough on the president but wanted to be passing legislation that fit their agenda more than chasing strange and hard to prove conspiracy theories about the president.

So, when we arrived back in DC, it should be noted that apart from a few more scheduled showing hearings, there was nothing on the Judiciary Committee agenda except sulking that they did not get what they wanted from the spring of discontent with the Mueller report.

It was not for lack of trying, but Nadler's desire to relitigate the Mueller investigation was never-ending and with disastrous backlash on his own team. So as the festering of impeachment was still being plotted behind the scenes by Adam Schiff, Chairman Nadler called Corey Lewandowsky to testify about his involvement in the Mueller report on September 17, 2019. By now I was just wondering if this was just a real-life re-creation of the cartoon featuring the Road Runner and Wile E. Coyote. With Wile E. Coyote planning his sure-fire plan to get the Road Runner only to fall victim to his own trap every time. With Lewandowsky, what Nadler thought would be an easy media hit became just another fiasco because in this witness they had called someone who wanted to be there and had no problem going after the committee that called him. Another popcorn committee moment was teed up and ready to go, while the storm was building in another part of the building.

September 17, 2019, arrived with the Democrats on the Judiciary still hell-bent on finding a way to bring down President Trump. They had no idea what they wanted to do, but they seemed to feel that even though Robert Mueller himself had cast doubt on their theories they seemed to think if they just read out loud more of the report that it would finally, somehow magically seem different. In fact, the committee was so desperate, that we had to go through a hearing in which we changed the rules to allow staff questioning of witnesses. The problem was the staff on the Democratic side was so enamored with this concept that they failed to see that their definition of staff allowed almost everyone in the room to be considered staff except elected members of Congress. So today would be the day that Barry Berke would take center stage playing his part in begging the American public to believe they really had something that was impeachable on this president.

I will say before we go on, Barry Berke and Norm Eisen are two immensely powerful and successful Democrat attorneys brought in at the beginning of Congress to handle what Jerry Nadler believed would be the impeachment of Donald Trump. The problem Chairman Nadler had was that through Democrat bumbling with their approach and the fact that the Mueller report did not provide what they thought it would regarding impeachment, they were stuck with two particularly good attorneys who had not been able to shine publicly, which is the main reason they would take time out of lucrative practices in private life to be a part of this circus that unfolded in the Judiciary Committee. On a personal note, I enjoyed my interactions with them. However, their brilliance outside the committee and their relative lack of knowledge on how the committee operated led to many of the fights, and I believe the perception problems the Democrats had faced all year in this committee would cost them more as the year rolled on. We would see much more of these two as the year progressed, but at this point, as later, they tried to provide gravitas to the proceedings on the Democrat side. But even their fine legal skills could not make a case where one just did not exist, and the heavy-handed influence on the committee and especially the Democratic staff led the majority down some bad choices that I, as the ranking member, was happy to allow them to go down. In the end, it just made my case stronger as to the sham this had become.

Having Barry Berke doing the questioning was as much for show as it was to protect their own members, who did not think they could ask good questions of the witnesses. It also was designed to provide the optic that was not possible in a five-minute line of questioning by members, which is standard. By allowing thirty minutes of uninterrupted questions by a seasoned hired gun, they could paint a narrative pointing the audience in the way they wanted them to go. The one thing they did not expect was a witness who was not only itching for a fight but who came prepared to bring the fight to the Democrats. Mr. Lewandowsky was aggressive from the start, forcing the Democrats away from their talking points and making him the center of attention. For the most part, they never laid a glove on him in any real way. The mainstream media was disappointed, and the headlines just echoed what was becoming a known fact on the Hill: Chairman Nadler was desperate and did not have a clue as how to reach his goal of getting President Trump.

During my opening statement, I expressed my feelings about the whole affair:

> Mr. Chairman, there is so much we could actually do together. There is so much. But as long as we don't have time, we'll continue with rerun season. Popcorn still tastes good. I do not know why we do this except maybe we just have—maybe a deficiency of flash-bulbs. I do not know. Because we just like the show.

It is important to note that it was not just me who saw the futility of the majority's obsession. Jerry Nadler realized it too. In a quote to the *New York Daily News* the day before the Lewandowsky hearing he said, "If you are going to impeach the president, you want more than Democrats and Progressives to understand what you are doing.... You must have enough public support so that you are not tearing the country apart, so that you don't have half the country saying for the next 30 years, 'We won the election, you stole in from us.'"

Little did he know how prophetic those words would be as time played out. What they unleashed was not moving anyone except the members of their choir. This was a lonely bus the chairman could not find a way to get off.

The hearing played out just as I had predicted, and at the end of the day, the Democrats cried victory. Bending the rules of the committee to allow staff to ask questions added some drama but made no real difference. As I walked back to my office that night, I could not help but be struck at how desperate this all was becoming. I could not get the chairman to move on. He was stuck in this pipe dream of Mueller and continuing to investigate an issue that most of America had decided they did not care about anymore. In Washington, men and women leave their homes and families each week to pursue what they believe, or thought they believed, is a noble purpose. On that night, walking back to my office, I really had to question what we were doing and how much longer it would last.

What we did not know at the time was that behind the scenes and about to spill over into the real battle of the fall was the whistleblower report on the call from back in July. I knew that Chairman Nadler had for the most part lad the committee down a bad road in which even members of his own party had lost faith in his and the committee's ability to handle the business of the committee. What I did not know at the time, but would soon discover, was that while Jerry Nadler was chasing shadows trying to get results, Chairman Adam Schiff was preparing to move into the spotlight. All through the year, Schiff had been the better chairman as far as getting information and witnesses because he understood that you need to work with people to get what you want, a good mix of sweet and salty. Chairman Nadler only understood the old paradigm of leadership: brute force and subpoenas. In the end, that approach had left empty witness chairs and little to show for his efforts. So, while we were having a show hearing with Corey Lewandowsky, Jerry Nadler was being cut out of the loop for the next phase of this circus. Chairman Nadler would have a part to play as the rest of this impeachment drama played out, but his old school ways would be supplanted by the slick operator from California, Adam Schiff.

To gain perspective about what went on in the fall of 2019, you have to understand that in my mind there were two distinct dramas playing out. The one that most people saw was the one over a phone call that President Trump made to the Ukrainian President Zelensky. Now if you were a Democrat out to get Donald Trump, you would jump at any opportunity, and the media-savvy Adam Schiff was ready to take the paper-thin case that the president did something wrong and milk it for all it was worth. As you remember, a hidden secret of this circus was that Adam Schiff was not just a member of Congress who chaired the Intelligence Committee, but he was also a fact witness to this case because of his involvement with the whistleblower. Adam Schiff dragged the country along with him as he attempted to make a case out of a phone call. That is the first story of the fall of 2019.

The other story is the one that, long after the headlines had been written and the impeachment was done, I witnessed firsthand and the one I believe did the most damage to our democracy. I believe that President Donald Trump did nothing wrong on the call when taken in context and at the end of the day the charge was leveled from a political vendetta perspective not a true criminal one. The president did as he should have—he fought—and I believe, deep down, most saw the factual case for what it was: NOTHING. The other story that I believed damaged America is the absolute abuse of power that came from Speaker Nancy Pelosi, Majority Leader Steny Hoyer, Chairman Jerry Nadler, the Democrats as a whole, and, most importantly, Chairman Adam Schiff. So as the story of the clock and calendar turns to the final stretch, the facts are rather simple and easy to explain. The process for how they carried it out should scare everyone. It is that story that I cannot let go untold.

As we look at the events surrounding the events of that fall, two quotes from Professor Johnathan Turley of George Washington University stick out and should be the basis for viewing these events. The first quote was from his opening statement to the Judiciary Committee during impeachment when he said, "If the House proceeds solely on the Ukrainian allegations, this impeachment would stand out among modern impeachments as the shortest proceeding, with the thinnest evidentiary record, and the narrowest grounds ever used to impeach a president. That does not bode well for future presidents who are working in a country often sharply and, at times, bitterly divided."

Turley was commenting on the fact that the allegations lacked the standing of impeachment.

Turley's other quote strikes at the heart of my concern for this time in our history. When talking about the charge of obstruction of Congress, Turley said, "Basing impeachment on this obstruction theory would itself be an abuse of power…by Congress."

So here we are with a case that does not meet the standard for any criminality, much less impeachment, and a Congress that is abusing its power. We can never think that the American people do not get what the Democrat did to them. In this case, they wasted their tax dollars to try and remove a president they did not like to win the presidential election the next year. In the end, all they did was damage democracy.

The transcript of the call made by the president on July 25, the day after Robert Mueller's hearing in the House, had been circulating around the Inspector General Office of the intelligence community for most all of August. It was filed on August 12, 2019, by an anonymous third party who was told of the call by someone who was on the call. The report stated that the president was pressuring the Ukrainian president to help by investigating a rival of the president in the next election cycle, former Vice President Joe Biden. The report outlined the ways in which they believed the president was pressuring the Ukrainian president and that it was a matter of urgent attention. The report was inflamed by the fact that the administration in mid-July held up funds that were set aside for the Ukrainian military. It was also found out later that the whistleblower had met with Adam Schiff and his staff prior to making the complaint. But on the reporting form, a whistleblower is instructed to indicate whether or not they have had any contact with Congress about the allegations, and this whistleblower did not check either box. So, the call that started it all led to a report that before it was filed was probably discussed with a man who had sighted in on conspiracy by the president for over two years, when it involved the Russia investigation and the resulting Mueller investigation.

Before this became public knowledge in September, Adam Schiff and his merry band of staffers had almost a month of knowledge of and help, it appears, in drafting the report that was turned in. The unfortunate part, but not very surprising, was that Adam Schiff denied his part in it and was even called out by the *Washington Post* for his lies. The report was first made public on September 13, 2019, when Adam Schiff subpoenaed the report for Acting Director of National Intelligence Joseph Maguire. At first, it appeared proper enough—a committee chairman asking for documents within his committee's purview—but it appeared in hindsight now that a month after the report was filed, this was the way they were going to get it out in the open so the American public could see it. It was now coming together:

by having assisted the whistleblower in making the report, they knew how to follow up on it, and if it became stuck, then they would know exactly where to go and how to get it.

The whistleblower report is supposed to be shared with Congress if it is deemed credible by the intelligence community and the inspector general. In this case, Michael Atkinson, the IG investigated the report and deemed it to be an urgent credible matter. He then forwarded it to the acting DNI Joseph Maguire, who typically would forward the report to the intelligence committees on the Hill. However, in this case he said he would not turn it over because in his estimation the disclosure in this case did not concern allegations of conduct by a member of the intelligence community or involve an intelligence activity under the DNI's supervision. It was after a request for the report by Adam Schiff, who, of course, knew of the report, that the denial was made. Then Adam Schiff not only subpoenaed the report but also had Maguire come in and testify. Now, by this time, things about the report were starting to leak out, and it was becoming known that there was something that happened on a call that the president had with the Ukrainian president. As the rumors began to circulate, it appears Adam Schiff started using his position to make this the next scandal that would harm the president, and he was going to be in charge. What came next was a week that should have put this faux scandal to rest but instead lit the flame on the whole story.

On September 24, 2019, Speaker Nancy Pelosi did what many had been hoping for but did not think she would do: she announced that the House would be opening a formal impeachment proceeding against the president of the United States. As are most things that the Speaker does, especially when it dealt with President Trump, it was overly dramatic and very wrong. While I sat in the Judiciary Committee library room listening to her with my staff, the first thing that came to my mind had nothing to do with the facts or lack of them regarding an impeachment. It had to do with the fact that the Speaker cannot declare by her words that the House was now conducting an impeachment proceeding. As much power as the Speaker thought she may have, this was not one of them. The power of impeachment lies in the vote of the House as a whole and not in one person, even if they are the Speaker.

I had spent my whole time in the House learning the rules and how to apply them, so while everyone was worrying about how this would play out, I stuck to my guns and kept hammering the fact that this was a fake impeachment. I had been dealing with that line all year and winning because no matter how much you want to wish it so, until you follow proper procedure it is just a game. Minority Leader Kevin McCarthy called a meeting with the other ranking members to discuss what to do. After a lot of discussion, my recommendation was to not play the game. Go on the offense and make them explain why they are not following proper procedure and that they can do this all they want but, in the end, it will not lead to impeachment because, at this time, the Democrats were not serious. They just wanted the show. The best way to disrupt the play is to pull the curtain back and turn on the lights so you can see the stage is empty.

What happened next was classic Donald Trump. He would never be one to be bested in the public arena, and he knew how to command attention. The day after Speaker Pelosi said she was opening an impeachment inquiry based on this supposedly corrupt call, the president announced that he would release the transcript of the call because he said the call was "perfect, no problems at all." The game was on, and the president was not going to take it lying down. Pelosi had better come with more than a threat of a fake impeachment process.

The next day was one of the most unusual days of my time in Congress. We were called to the White House to be briefed on the transcript of the declassified call that was going to be released. The announcement by Speaker Pelosi the day before that she was going to just—poof—out of thin air begin an impeachment inquiry was what I often refer to as being too cute by half. In other words, she was pushing the narrative that the president had committed an impeachable offense, and she just expected everyone to agree with her version of the story. What she did not anticipate was that the president would release the transcript of the call. So no longer could she hide behind being able to only share her version of events. This was a game changer and made me think of my mom's old saying that if you have a big decision, wait twenty-four hours and make sure you have thought of all possibilities. In this case, if she had, the whole situation may have turned out differently. But once she committed, she was trapped in her decision. So that morning, as members of both the House and Senate were called to the White House to be briefed on the transcript, it was with a great sense of anticipation to see what all the fuss was about. I remember sitting in the Roosevelt Room with these other members, thinking, *What could possibly be in this call that would be worthy of impeachment?* I had hoped we were beyond this, but here we were. After we all were in the room, a member of the White House Counsel's office stated that the president had declassified the call and was going to release the transcript publicly to show that there was nothing in the call that was bad, much less impeachable. We were then handed a copy of the transcript, and we all began to read.

Now I have always been a fast reader, so I read through the call, and when I got to the end, I was stunned. Surely this was just part of the call. Surely there was something else that would have caused this much controversy. I also had that feeling that maybe I just did not read it right, so while everyone else was reading through it, I quickly read it again. I knew we would be asked for our thoughts, and I did not want to be embarrassed by not picking up on something that was obvious to the others in the room. After a while, you could tell by the shuffling in the chairs that people were finishing up reading the transcript. It was in that awkward moment when no one seemed to know what to do that somebody—and I wish I could remember which member it was because it is too funny not to properly quote, but I cannot—asked rather matter-of-factly whether we were sure the president was on this call because the language was too clean. For a moment, the room was silent. Then someone else chimed in, saying they thought the same thing, and the room started laughing. We did not take lightly the trouble that was being caused by the call, but we also could not believe this was what the Democrats were going to base an impeachment inquiry on. The call did not reveal any corruption or overtly bad acts. It was a call that should have gained no traction at all, except that someone on the call decided this, if spun properly, could be used to get the president, and they began to share with some not on the call. It was their sharing, and I believe their desire to get another swipe at the president, that led to the report.

I was sitting at the end of the long conference table in the Roosevelt Room, and Pat Cippolini, the president's White House counsel, came in while I was reading and sat down. I had gotten to know Pat somewhat over the last few months dealing with all the misadventures in the Judiciary Committee. Pat was the perfect person for this time in the White House. He was levelheaded and smart as a whip, and had gathered a solid team of lawyers around him to defend this White House against the constant barrage of attacks by the Democrats. I always admired that he never seemed to get flustered. He was always listening and then asking the right question to know how best to respond. That morning, you could see in his face he was tired. The last year would take it out of anyone with the normal responsibilities as White House counsel, but lay on top of all that the craziness coming from Speaker Pelosi, Chairman Nadler, and Chairman Adam Schiff and you understood why he looked a little worn down. I looked at him while some others were talking, and I asked him if this was it. He looked up and said yes. I said this must be a joke. Speaker Pelosi wanted to impeach over this transcript? It did not make sense. Pat shook his head and agreed and made the profound point that if she had just waited twenty-four hours, she could have made an educated decision about what she wanted to do but instead chose to go forward without seeing the evidence. I just shook my head as well and told him that after this was all over, we were going to have to sit down over a quiet meal and talk. He just laughed and said you would not believe the half of it. Little did I know that after that day, he and I would talk regularly as we had to defend against the sham impeachment that was brewing on Capitol Hill.

Later that day, the transcript was released, and the reaction was predictable. If you were a Democrat thinking that the president was bad no matter what he did, then you found the transcript full of threats and coercion. If you came at it from a neutral position, or at least an open mind, you could see that the call was not what it was made out to be. You might not like what the president had asked about—namely, Joe Biden and the Ukrainian corruption investigations—but it was weak on trying to show the president had committed any crime. It was not a call that should have triggered an impeachment inquiry, even the fake one that the Speaker had announced the day before. Still, here we were, moving headlong into an investigation, all because Democrats were mad that the Mueller report was a flop, and they needed to get to this president. The election cycle was starting up, and they were desperate to find a way to help whoever won on their side in the primaries win the general election and defeat President Trump. The problem they had was that even worse than before, the clock and calendar were growing short of time.

As we proceeded down the path that the Democrats were laying out, it became clear after the release of the transcript they would have to prove to the American people—and, to be honest, some of their own members—why this was impeachable. They would have to lay out a plan that was unique and quick. In fact, it would be the fastest ever impeachment. If they were going to get this done and over to the Senate by the first of the year, they would have to not just bend the rules but break them. And they may even need to make up a few along the way. As this investigation played out, it would be clear that the Democrats came into this year with two parts of a plan already established: motive and opportunity. Their motive was to make sure they could influence the 2020 election so that President Trump could not win reelection, and the best way to do that was to remove him. Remember that Speaker Pelosi had made it clear that she was not a fan of the president. The Speaker now had the ability to make life hard on the president, and no one doubted that she and the Democrats would do all in their power to follow through on their threats of investigations and possibly impeachment. They also now had opportunity. Since they took the majority, they controlled the machine in the House, and it allowed them to move forward with the investigation.

However, from where I was sitting, they were still missing one leg of the stool—means. The one thing that the phone call presented to them was the ability to try and spin their narrative apart from law enforcement or outside meddling in the interpretation of the facts. They had a chairman in Adam Schiff who had already shown he was willing to play fast and loose with the facts. Remember him saying several times with no proof to back it up that collusion between the president and

Russia was in plain sight? Adam Schiff was about to put his best lawyering together to use the call to build his own case against Donald Trump. So now they had it: the three-legged stool was complete in their minds. They had motive, they had opportunity, and they had the means. All they had to do was break some rules and control the narrative, and they could succeed.

What came next will forever in my mind change not only the discussion of impeachment but the very fabric that has kept the House of Representatives going for over 200 years. The desire to win at all costs would drive the country and our institution to its breaking point. The use of a House majority to inflict political damage of this magnitude was unimaginable just a few short years ago. Republicans and Democrats have always used the majority's power to pass partisan agenda items; it is the perk of the majority. The difference in what was about to transpire was the blatant manipulation of the rules of the House that had kept us a legislative body since the inception of our country. However we got here, the truth was we were here, and there was no turning back.

The only question for us became how they would attempt to carry it out. The means was a phone call that by even the most partisan interpretation was troubling but not enough in most minds to bring us to the height of legislative power in the system of checks and balances that our country was founded on: impeachment of the head of the executive branch. At the beginning of the Congress, Speaker Pelosi had said of impeachment that if it were to happen it would need to be bipartisan and obvious enough that the American people would be supportive of the process. With the year winding down and no other options available to get at the president, Speaker Pelosi and her leadership abandoned their noble principles of the past. They now had what they thought was the perfect stool: motive, opportunity, and means. And they were not about to let this moment pass.

The big question that Republican members had in this process was what the role of the Judiciary would be in this sham. The interesting thing from my perspective during this whole year was that everything on the Democratic side of the aisle had to be a group project. It almost felt like they were in kindergarten again and everything had to be done as a group to keep people from getting their feelings hurt. Since the start of the Congress, Speaker Pelosi had always talked about and instructed that multiple committees were to carry out this investigation of the president. You had Judiciary, Intel, House Oversight and Reform, Ways and Means, Financial Services, and Foreign Affairs all tasked with investigating President Trump with the idea of finding something to impeach him with. No one thought this would be workable; other ranking members, including me, thought if this what they wanted to do, fine. It was so spread out that nothing would get done, and we could see that the infighting between Democratic chairmen was slowing down the investigation. What we did not know until the Speaker announced the impeachment inquiry had started was how these committees would all play together. To keep the peace in her caucus, the Speaker made a call that will forever taint these proceedings and lend them even greater illegitimacy. She stated that the Intel Committee, led by Chairman Adam Schiff, would oversee these hearings and that the Foreign Affairs Committee and House Oversight and Reform Committee members would be allowed to join in these hearings. These initial hearings were going to be conducted not out in the open but behind closed doors and without representation for the president of the United States. It was just the beginning of a long fall that would see House rules and decorum shredded.

The one thing that jumped out at me during this process was that the Judiciary Committee was left out of the process. We were marginalized and left watching the show play out in another committee, with no input from the one committee whose job it is to handle impeachment. When I asked Chairman Nadler what was going on, I would either get a muttered non-acknowledgment of my question or I would get an indignant response, claiming that the investigation was going on, and that we would be involved at some point. I was frustrated because I had sat in a committee that was (and I still believe is) the best committee on the Hill. It has a large jurisdictional reach, and when guarded it would rival the Energy and Commerce committee in terms of relevance on most issues going through the House. Now we were on the sidelines because for most of the year, the chairman and his committee members decided that instead of acting like members of Congress and trying to get things done, they would act as if the rules did not apply to them and that they would do or say whatever they wanted as long as it fulfilled one of two goals: attack President Donald Trump and pass partisan bills that had no hope of becoming law but played well to the liberal base that elected them. The showboating, the name-calling, and the theatrics, such as the fried chicken stunt, had left our committee damaged among Democrats. The moderate part of the Democratic majority wanted nothing to do with the juvenile stunts that were going on in Judiciary. Democratic members of the House would come to me all the time and ask if it was as off the rails as it appeared. I would simply tell them it was worse than you could imagine. The disdain for the process exhibited by the chairman and the Democrats on the committee had forced the leadership in the House, along with Speaker Pelosi, to remove the committee from the front lines of this stage of the impeachment, which was still not a valid impeachment inquiry.

One thing was true: the Judiciary Committee was benched, and Adam Schiff was firmly in control. He had worked all year to find a way to rise to this spot, and with the whistleblower report and the ability (it appeared) to coach the whistleblower to get this call public, he was now in the driver's seat. He had wrested control away from Jerry Nadler and was preparing for his time to take down President Trump. He would do it all from his classified perch in the Intel Committee offices and away from the prying eyes of the media. I guess if you want to form the narrative to suit your purposes, then it is nice to have your own government-funded star chamber where you are the judge, the jury, and, hopefully, the executioner. Welcome to the Democratic majority!

As we went through the month of October, it was apparent that the Schiff Show was desperate to find anything that it could use to show that the president did something inappropriate on the call. To accomplish this, Schiff kept the hearings closed to the public, limited the questioning of the minority members, and then after threatening the Republican members of the committee with Ethics Committee referrals to keep them from talking, he and other Democrats would go to the press and spin the hearings as they wanted them to be reported. The leaks were the thing that kept the press's interest high and assured him that he would have fawning coverage of whatever he gave the media. The minority side was limited in their participation in the proceedings, and through it all the Judiciary Committee, where impeachment is supposed to be found, was kept at arm's length. It was during these hearings that we were introduced to witnesses like Lt. Col. Alexander Vindman, Fiona Hill, Marie Yovanovitch, George Kent, and William Taylor. These names and others were to become fixtures in the October secret hearings and then in the public hearings in November.

The problems that we had experienced all year in the Judiciary Committee, however, would be the star of the show in these hearings as well. For the Democrats' antics and utter disregard for procedure and process were to doom these hearings long before they tried to make their case to the world. I had been on the receiving end of the majority's abuse in the hearings we had been having all year, but where Jerry Nadler was heavy-handed and came off many times as just belligerent in his ways, Adam Schiff was a character of another level. He was very polished in his presentation, and even when spouting falsehoods—such as there was evidence in plain sight of collusion between President Trump and the Russians—he could come off as very calm and reasonable. It was that almost psychotic calmness that made Speaker Pelosi, who had grown weary of Jerry Nadler, tap him to lead this final last-gasp attempt to get President Trump. Adam Schiff also had the advantage of being chairman of a committee that had a history of bipartisan, out-of-the-press work. The committee's work was often not televised due to the nature of the classified information that the committee handled.

So, when the Speaker saw the opportunity to use Schiff for the hearings due to the whistleblower complaint coming from the intelligence community, she jumped at the chance. If she was going to deliver to her caucus the goal of getting Donald Trump, she was going to place all her cards in her friend from California and then sit back as he took that hand and spun a web that all but ensured that the impeachment of Donald Trump would become a reality. The original pronouncement by Speaker Pelosi that a formal impeachment inquiry was to begin, as I said earlier, was nothing more than a press release. It did not, in the end, signify any more power for the committees to do their work. It just made a formal distinction that was as much of a slap at the Judiciary Committee and its chairman as it was a call to impeachment. The underlying thought was that the Judiciary Committee could not handle this investigation and that they needed someone who could present a better picture to the public about what they were doing and do so with an iron hand that would not be seen. She got both in Adam Schiff.

While the hearings got started in the basement hearing rooms of the Intel Committee, I called my staff together and laid out what I thought would happen and how we should respond. I knew that if at some point they were going to make this a formal inquiry, we would need to be ready because as much as I knew Speaker Pelosi wanted to make this happen, she was not going to bypass the Judiciary Committee altogether. She would just simply have it all wrapped up and given to the Judiciary Committee to finalize and bring to the floor. I had our investigative staff communicate with the Intel staff as to the latest developments, and I would meet with our members who were on the other committees who were allowed in the room to question these witnesses. What came out of those discussions cemented in my mind that the Democrats were willing to go to any extreme to get Donald Trump.

The October inquisition would be a media circus with discussion of everyone who testified and the inevitable Adam Schiff press availability, during which he would frame the narrative of the testimony. The reality was that in the room Adam Schiff was running a tight ship. He would insert himself into the testimony, and by stopping Republican lines of questioning—a habit that would come back to bite him when these hearings went public—he would keep certain facts from being introduced or challenged. The tempers in the room were always on edge with the Republicans fuming and members chafing against the star chamber quality of the proceedings. The frustrations came to a head on October 23, 2019. Many of my Republican colleagues were frustrated about the way the proceedings were going and decided to make a stand and proceed into the closed hearing so they could witness for themselves what was going on. Of course, Adam Schiff just adjourned the meeting and refused to go on until he could be alone in the basement to continue the hearings. After about a five-hour delay the hearing continued, and the Democrats kept up the march toward impeachment.

Now some might be asking themselves why this mattered. Just because the Democrats were acting inappropriately, there was no reason for the Republicans to follow them down that path. I would disagree—when you continue to push and crowd out a minority party and, at the same time, break long-standing rules and traditions for the sake of getting your way, giving the minority no opportunity to gain relief, the minority must act. The pushing of their way into the proceedings highlighted several things that should have never been allowed. There is a rule of the House that says that any member of the House can request to see transcripts and other materials from any hearing of a House committee. In this case, because they wanted to keep everything to themselves and only show what they had to, the Democrats stated that they were not going to allow this practice for these proceedings. This is just a blatant violation of House rules with no consequence. They also were not allowing duly elected members of the House to sit in on the meetings, which, again, is a violation of long-standing House decorum.

The question became: What are you hiding, and why are you running over the rights of fellow elected members of Congress? The answer was simple, and, thus, why I felt my colleagues were justified in acting out against the oppressive nature of these proceedings. It was a sham that was being perpetrated, and the House and the president of the United States were being railroaded at the whim of Chairman Schiff and Speaker Pelosi. The procedural atrocities that the Democrats used that fall are the lasting remnants of this time, and I believe strike at the very core of a workable Congress. If members do not feel they are able to perform their job because of the tyranny of the majority, America will get a dysfunctional and ineffective body. It is one thing to pull these kinds of stunts when dealing with legislation, but when you are recklessly wielding the power of impeachment, you are cutting at the very fabric of democracy. To the Democrats out to get President Trump, that was a price they were willing to pay.

As the star chamber hearings were dragging on toward the end of October, you could sense a rise in tension within the Democratic

Caucus. I would ask Chairman Nadler and other Democratic members what was next and whether they had plans for what they were going to do, reminding them that whatever was going on the basement with the Intel Committee was a lot of things but a formal impeachment inquiry it was not. I had been saying this in internal GOP leadership meetings and in every interview that I had during this time. I had several reasons for keeping this up, not the least of which was that I was right. Another reason was simple fairness: if I could show that these meetings were being done without any sense of fairness, then even those Americans who were not fans of the president would be appalled. I knew that one thing Americans will not stand for is unfairness. Our country is based on the very premise that you are innocent until proven guilty, and the Democrats had tried to turn that storied principle on its head. My last reason was that I knew that the investigation was not going to show that the president had done anything wrong, much less impeachable, but the Democrats were going to Impeach Donald Trump no matter how weak the evidence was and then it would go to the Senate for a trial. When it made it to the Senate, I wanted to make sure that the record was preserved to show that this was not only a vengeance-filled investigation, but also one in which the very basics of fairness were trampled on. So as October drew to a close you could feel the panic growing. The Democrats had to do something fast if they were going to try and impeach the president before the end of the year and not have it look even more like a rush job. The reality was they were long past that, but they needed a new coat of paint and a plan. That was why on October 31, 2019, the House formally approved a plan for impeachment proceedings that were unlike anything this country has ever seen.

Halloween was in full force in 2019 on the House floor. Speaker Pelosi, after claiming that her actions on September 24 had called the House into an impeachment inquiry, had to backtrack and admit she was wrong. Now I wish I could say that she had the honesty to do that, but she did not. She instead had Congressman Jim McGovern draw up what would become known as House Resolution 660, which was supposed to be the formal way for the House to proceed with the impeachment investigation. The procedure that was laid out was one of expediency, not fairness. For example, the president and his team at the White House did not even had a part in the process until it came to the Judiciary Committee and then, and only at the consent of the chairman, could the president have a viable way of defending himself. It was this lack of transparency and formal involvement that led the president's team to not participate in the hearings. There was literally nothing for them to participate in. Kevin McCarthy, who was the minority leader, said, "It's been 34 days since Nancy Pelosi unilaterally declared her impeachment inquiry. Today's backtracking is an admission that this process has been botched from the start. We will not legitimize the Schiff, Pelosi sham impeachment." The Democrats were on a timetable, and they would not listen to reason.

The rules were thrown together to give the appearance of fairness, but without offering any. Speaker Pelosi, in about as close to an admission she would give, said this in a letter about the vote she was calling for: "For weeks, the President, his Counsel in the White House, and his allies in Congress have made the baseless claim that the House of Representatives' impeachment inquiry 'lacks the necessary authorization for a valid impeachment proceeding.' They argue that, because the House has not taken a vote, they may simply pretend the impeachment inquiry does not exist." She went on to say, "This week, we will bring a resolution to the Floor that affirms the ongoing, existing investigation that is currently being conducted by our committees as part of this impeachment inquiry."

The bold indifference to the blatant trashing of House rules for a political end would have been abhorrent to the founders of our Republic. Yet here we were, and with the clock ticking they had to have a process to point to in order to save face.

That morning when I took to the floor to talk about this resolution I felt a mix of frustration, anger, and sadness. I was not managing the resolution on the floor since it came out of the Rules Committee instead of the Judiciary Committee, but it just goes to show how far out of favor Chairman Nadler had fallen with his antics that year in the judiciary committee. He had so embarrassed the committee that the Speaker could not even let the resolution setting up what would be the impeachment procedure come from the committee that should and would be handling the impeachment. Now as an aside, my staff and the chairman's staff did not agree on a lot of things but the idea that the intel committee was leading the charge on this impeachment was repugnant to both sides in the Judiciary Committee. Unfortunately, they could not see that they were their own worst enemies. As I walked to the floor with my notes that the staff had drawn up, I was wondering whether we could ever find a good way out of this and whether we could go back to normal and work for the folks who sent us to Washington. Right then, the only thing the Democrats really wanted to do was impeach this president, no matter what it took.

When I took to the floor to discuss the bill, I challenged the process that was being used. I pointed out that if this had been an honest project the chairman of the Rules Committee, James P. McGovern (D-MA), would have known that the resolution we were voting on establishing protocols for public hearings did not even outline a procedure for the work product of the Intel Committee to be turned over to the House Judiciary Committee for processing into an actual impeachment resolution. It turned out that I should not have been too concerned about the format because in the end it would not matter anyway as we would not follow this resolution. It really was sad when you think about it. I waited on the floor that day listening to members speak and I thought to myself, *Why are we doing this and spending this much time and energy?* My subconscious reminded me that this was not about anything except extracting a price on a president they did not like, so in the end all this was foreplay to the ultimate act of impeachment. In other words, pay no attention the black cloud descending around the House. You are to only pay attention to the things we were not, and if a president was caught up in that so be it.

After the vote on the floor, which was bipartisan against the proceedings, the Republicans had a press conference to talk about what had just happened. I knew that eventually this would come to us in Judiciary they could not sideline us forever, and I intended to put the Democrats on notice that if is the way you wanted to play so be it, I was ready for the fight and Adam Schiff needed to know I was going to pin the blame on him. At the press conference, I laid it out noticeably clear that if Mr. Schiff was going to be the leader, he would have to act like one. I said:

> Folks, this ain't over. Get ready. I tell you what, when it gets to the Judiciary Committee, I do have one thing for Mr. Schiff, "Come to the Judiciary Committee. Be the first witness and take every question asked of you. Starting with your own involvement with the whistleblower.

I wish I could say that Adam Schiff rose to the occasion, but in the end, he played the part of the kid in class who was always stirred up trouble but only when no one was looking and who always succeeded in getting someone else in trouble. Adam Schiff wanted the glory but none of the work. After the vote on October 31, 2019, the stage was set to cherry-pick his witnesses for the public part of the impeachment hearings, which were to start in a matter of days. For the time being we could only watch from the Judiciary perspective, but we knew the train was on the track, and we knew it would get to us soon. So, while we waited, we tried to prepare for what lay ahead.

Now in reading this account it should be evident we were not dealing with a normal impeachment process. This was not like in *All the President's Men,* where a long-drawn-out investigation of President Nixon lasting for several years ended with a lot of evidence that the president had committed criminal acts that required impeachment. Not only had there been a lot of investigations into Watergate going on outside Capitol Hill, but both the Senate and the House had engaged in extensive investigations. It was also not like the impeachment of President Clinton, which had originated from investigations surrounding certain of his activities that had been going on for years. It also should be noted that in each of these cases the president and his team were represented in the process and given access to defend themselves all along the way. No, the Trump impeachment proceeding was what the Founders had feared: a political impeachment.

Alexander Hamilton wrote in *The Federalist Papers: #65* that there was a distinct fear that impeachment could become a partisan exercise, warning that impeachment:

> ...will seldom fail to agitate the passions of the whole community, and to divide it into parties more or less

friendly or inimical to the accused. In many cases it will connect itself with the pre-existing factions, and will enlist all their animosities, partialities, influence, and interest on one side or on the other; and in such cases there will always be the greatest danger that the decision will be regulated more by the comparative strength of parties, than by the real demonstrations of innocence or guilt.

A political impeachment is one that is not founded on the idea that a president did something that was illegal or threatened the integrity of the office; a political impeachment is one that is grounded in the belief that when you have the power to implement a political outcome you should use it for that purpose. People will argue that the Mueller investigation showed that the president committed impeachable offenses, but in the end it did not, and the Democrats knew this as well. The Ukrainian phone call that the nation was being told was the cause of this recent wave of hearings also did not present the basis for impeachment, but it did give the Democrats an excuse for trying to convince Americans that they were being thorough and were simply holding the president accountable. Even if you were inclined to believe that, the process and speed of this impeachment just does not meet with the factual reality that they were desperate, and time was running out. This was the best they had, and it was what they would use no matter what the facts said.

A member of Congress once made the following observation about impeachment—an observation that certainly fit the situation we were seeing play out in real time:

> There must never be a narrowly voted impeachment or an impeachment supported by one of our major political parties and opposed by another. Such an impeachment will produce divisiveness and bitterness in politics for years to come and will call into question the very legitimacy of our political institutions.

This member went on to warn, "The American people are watching, and they will not forget. You may have the votes, you may have the muscle, but you do not have the legitimacy of a national consensus or of a constitutional imperative. This partisan coup-d'état will go down in infamy in the history of this nation."

Now you may be thinking that came from me or another Republican talking about the Trump impeachment, but you would be wrong. Those words came from the mouth of Jerry Nadler in a speech on the House floor during the Clinton impeachment. The interesting thing to me was that he seemed to forget that the public was still watching and what he and Adam Schiff and the Democrats were doing were nowhere close to the Clinton investigation. They did not have the time, and so the best thing to do was to forget what they once believed and push forward no matter what.

November opened with public hearings by the Intel Committee with a group of cherry-picked witnesses from Adam Schiff all designed to try and bolster their case. This would be a good time to pause for just a moment and remind you that this is not how it was ever supposed to be done. By the time Nancy Pelosi admitted that they made a mistake, and the House was not in actual impeachment mode and passed HR 660, the die was set and with barely a month of meetings supposedly investigating the facts in the case, they were ready to try and convince the American people. The clock and the calendar are oppressive task masters, but that is not the way it has always been. A look at the last two impeachment investigations will show that this one was not only lacking factually but, as I have emphasized, pushed forward by any means necessary, including trashing the rules and decorum of the House to get a desired result.

Using history as a guide, I want to remind you what we had seen in the past and show just unfair these proceedings were. During the investigation into President Nixon, a congressman from New Jersey named Peter Rodino was the chairman of the Judiciary Committee in the House. In a floor speech in February 1974, he said, "The sole power of impeachment carries with it the power to conduct a full and complete investigation of whether sufficient grounds for impeachment exist or not exist…" Chairman Rodino understood that when it comes to the matter of impeachment nothing short of an exhaustive investigation with all sides participating would be fit for impeachment.

Unfortunately, for not only President Trump but also the country this was not what happened during the Trump impeachment. Much was made during the debate of HR 660 that this resolution provided an abundance of proper procedure for the president, and Jim McGovern even said that it was even more than provided President Clinton. If it were not so problematic that would be laughable. Instead it was a falsehood made to cover up the shoddy process that we were living through daily.

The difference in this impeachment goes to show that the damage done was not just to the president but to the institution of Congress. The problem the Democrats had was they believed the president was guilty. There was never an admission by the Democrats that they could be wrong. They knew he was guilty of *something*; they just needed something to prove it. That thought by itself throws jurisprudence on in its head. In our country, the opposite is true: you are innocent until proven guilty. However, Nancy Pelosi said that if the president had anything exculpatory ("Mr. President, that means anything that shows you are innocent," she trolled), then he should make it known. The disrespect and sarcasm just dripped from these words. The American people understand fairness, and what was happening was not even close to fair.

As I noted above, there were many differences between this impeachment proceeding and those of Nixon and Clinton. But the most obvious one was that those impeachments were predicated on criminal acts, which is not true in the case of President Trump. These acts committed by former President Nixon were substantiated through years of investigating, not days. The Trump investigation was not predicated on actual information received, but instead, it was rushed by the calendar. The previous administrations had had the opportunity to cross-examine witnesses and to have their own counsel present at all public hearings. This was never afforded to the Trump administration in any meaningful way. The Trump administration was completely excluded from the process until the possibility for participation came at the Judiciary Committee. But without any witnesses to cross-examine, it was a rather useless offer. The lack of cross-examination was coupled with the inability on its own or through the committee process to call their own witnesses. We as members could ask for witnesses, but the right to call witnesses was at the discretion of the chairmen. Devin Nunes and I had our witness list rejected and even ridiculed because we had the audacity to ask for witnesses the majority deemed irrelevant to their stated purposes. In short, the procedural protections claimed by the majority were woefully short.

The Clinton counsel got to access all information presented to the grand jury with Ken Starr and to attend any meeting, even executive sessions. They were invited to respond to evidence received and testimony given. They would ask for the committee to receive additional evidence or testimony. They could question any witness called before the committee and raise objections relating to the examination of these witnesses. An example of how different the Trump impeachment was from the previous rules can in the following comparison. President Clinton's counsel was not only allowed to make an opening statement, but also called fourteen witnesses and gave a closing argument. They also cross-examined witnesses, even including Ken Starr, the special counsel. This would prove telling when I tried to call Adam Schiff, who publicly fashioned himself as an independent counsel. Schiff refused to testify, although it was he and his committee who wrote the report on which the impeachment would be based.

It should be noted that during the Clinton impeachment hearings, these requests by his counsel were made after the chairman of the Judiciary Committee, Henry Hyde (R-IL), had already announced his intention to mark up the articles of impeachment; the committee then delayed its work to accommodate the president's team request.

There is also the difference that the Trump impeachment proceedings had just been authorized but had been going on unauthorized for a month without any input from the administration. The last, and most damning to me as one with a front seat to the train wreck that was these hearings, was that in previous impeachment hearings committee members could bring in additional evidence for the committee to examine, and the chairman and the ranking member had subpoena power that was only subject to being overruled by a vote of the committee. We never had to worry about this because Chairman Nadler never afforded us the opportunity. Fairness and due process are not easy things to deal with when you are on the clock and you must proceed with very little evidence.

That was what we were faced with: a runaway majority that insisted that it must do its work and that nothing was to keep them from it, even simple things like due process and a modicum of fairness. It was on this playing field that public hearings began in the Intel Committee. As a reminder, this is highly unusual. Impeachment hearings are typically found in the Judiciary Committee, but since Speaker Pelosi had lost faith in Chairman Nadler, we would be relegated to watching the hearings and then left to simply take whatever the Intel Committee gave us, since time was running short and we would not have time to investigate ourselves. So, with the clock running, Chairman Adam Schiff gaveled the hearings to order.

It is still rather stunning to most of us on the Hill that Chairman Schiff was being given the lead in this investigation. He was the head of the Intel Committee and one of the fiercest critics of President Trump, but his committee had one of the smaller staffs and little exposure to the bright lights that were about to be shone on them. It was also genuinely concerning that he is also the same Adam Schiff who forever stamped these hearings as anything but fair when back on September 26, 2019, he started the hearing with the then-acting director of national intelligence with a parody of the call between President Trump and President Zelensky of Ukraine. This was many people's first real exposure to the brewing controversy, and instead of hearing the truth about the call, they got the Adam Schiff parody:

> It reads like a classic organized crime shakedown. Shorn of its rambling character and in not so many words, this is the essence of what the president communicates.... I hear what you want. I have a favor I want from you though. And I'm going to say this only seven times, so you better listen good. I want you to make up dirt on my political opponent, understand. Lots of it. On this and on that.

And with those words, Schiff showed that he did not have any type of open mind and, in fact, showed why the American people should not trust him. He deliberately gave a false interpretation of the call that was intended to make the call seem more than it was. I was used to Chairman Nadler giving his version of the story all year in our committee, but I will have to give Nadler credit that he gave his own spin on the facts but never resorted to outright distortion of known facts when making his attacks on the president. Adam Schiff had no shame, and it would be a stain on these already farcical proceedings. It can never be forgotten that in these hearings, Adam Schiff should have been considered a fact witness to these events. He had direct contact with the whistleblower and tried to hide that fact. Even the *Washington Post* was able to make a fair call on his claim that he and his staff had never heard from the whistleblower when the paper called his claim a "whopper" of a lie. So when the public phase of these hearings began, we knew that the die was cast and that the witnesses who would testify would only be the ones that the Democrats thought had auditioned best in the star chamber–style hearings that had just been conducted. It was high theater designed to do one thing: make the American people believe that the president had done something on that call that was, at best, unfit for the president and, as they would attempt to portray it, worthy of impeachment.

Over the next few weeks, I would watch as the show played out before the world, with Adam Schiff running the show. And as witnesses testified to their accounts of the situation in Ukraine and the issues around the call, it was very apparent that Schiff would not let this be a hearing in which fairness was given. Remember, we are still in the time in which President Trump and his team had no rights in the process at all. This was amplified more with every witness. It was not just that the Democrats wanted to control the hearings concerning the witnesses, but they also rejected most of the names on the witness list Devin Nunes, the ranking member of the Intel Committee, put forward for the hearings. The reason given by the majority in rejecting most of the requests was that they excluded witnesses who would steer the hearings away from the focus they wanted, which was the perceived wrongdoing by President Trump. This, again, showed that these hearings were not about answers but about results. The intended result for the Democrats was the impeachment of Donald Trump.

Now there will be many books and stories written about the events of this fall with in-depth discussion of what each witness said as they testified. Those who testified became momentary household names for members of the public who followed the hearings. Gordon Sondland, the US ambassador to the European Union, testified that he assumed that the aid was held up in expectation of an investigation. But on the other side, Ambassador Kurt Volker, who served as special envoy to Ukraine, stated that there was no linkage between a White House meeting and the Ukrainian action on the investigation. Ambassador Volker's assertion was backed up by Tim Morrison, the senior director for Europe and Russia on the White House Security Council, who laid out several items that showed just how weak this case was for the Democrats. Morrison, who was on the call, said nothing improper happened. His testimony showed that the interpretation of the call the Democrats had been pushing was contradicted by facts. Morrison, though, did give the hearing information about the Democrats' star witness, Lieutenant Colonel Vindman. He stated that he had had concerns about Vindman's judgment in this matter and had kept him out of the loop. He also reported that he did not trust Vindman. This was a blow to the Democrats. But believe me, they had the story, and they were sticking to it.

As I look back over these hearings and this time, it just reminds me that these hearings were a formality and rushed because the verdict was already in, and all they needed were a few facts for the file. This would be problematic by the time it got to us, but Adam Schiff did not care. His job was to deliver the ball to the Judiciary Committee, and that was what he did.

I freely admit that as it played out, I could not see how the Democrats ever intended to make a case with the facts and witnesses that they had. I kept thinking about prior impeachments and wondering if they really had so poor a case or if they were holding out. The reality was we were watching the last testimony from a fact witness in these hearings. You got the feeling that this whole impeachment was a stretch, and even public polling showed that people, once they saw what was going on, did not believe the Democrats' push was worth it.

What we did see in these public hearings, though, was what I maintain is the greatest damage done in the impeachment fiasco, outside the attempted tarnishing of President Trump, and that was the trashing of the institution of the House of Representatives. Adam Schiff made it clear early on that he was not concerned with hearing from the minority on this issue, and he would use the power of the gavel to enforce his version of fairness with an iron hand. He would cut off members of the minority during their questioning time, he would add his own take on the hearings in unprecedented closing statements at the end of each day's hearings, and he would coach the witnesses not to answer certain valid questions from the minority. The highlight in the struggle for fairness can be shown in one sequence that stood out as a prime example of the unfairness in the process laid out by the Democrats.

The Democrats' hypocrisy and unfair bias occurred a few times but were particularly obvious in the testimony of Lieutenant Colonel Vindman. The problems started when ranking member Devin Nunes was questioning Vindman about with whom he had shared his concerns about the phone call made by the president. Nunes asked, "What agency was the individual from?" At this point, Schiff jumped in, and in his overbearing manner, stopped Nunes even though it was Nunes's time to ask questions.

Schiff said, "We don't want to use these proceedings—"

Devin Nunes interrupted Schiff in an attempt to continue but was cut off. Schiff stated, "We need to protect the whistleblower. I want to make sure that there is no effort to oust the whistleblower through these proceedings. If the witness has a good-faith belief that this may reveal the identity of the whistleblower, that is not the purpose that we are here for, and I want to advise the witness accordingly."

It is amazing that in a hearing designed to get to the truth, the chairman of the committee would give a witness a "get out of answering questions free" card if he felt like it would be inappropriate to answer. It was also in this hearing that Schiff asserted that it was against federal law to reveal the name of the whistleblower. This is inaccurate. The whistleblower statute protects the whistleblower from retribution for coming forward. If it was never to be known who the whistleblower was, why would you build in all these protections to ensure that they suffer no harm for coming forward with the truth? But the truth has never been a strong guidepost for this chairman, and this would be no exception.

This was not the last time the interruptions came up. Later, in a sharp exchange Jim Jordan, a fellow Judiciary Committee member, asked Lieutenant Colonel Vindman if he was the leaker, citing Tim Morrison's previous testimony that he had questioned Vindman's judgment. Vindman got really indignant and insisted that he would never leak information and thought it was preposterous to ask. I find it funny that he was willing to be offended about being asked if he was the leaker but was very willing to express his beliefs about the phone call and his belief about the president's actions but not his own. As the exchange continued, with Jim also asking about the people Vindman may have talked with about the call, the chairman swooped in again to save the day. However, it is in this following exchange that Adam Schiff showed his true colors.

> *"Gentleman will suspend," Schiff told Jordan. "As I indicated before, this committee will not be used to out the whistleblower."*

> *"Mr. Chairman, I don't see how this is outing the whistleblower," countered Jordan. "The witness has testified in his deposition that he doesn't know who the whistleblower is. You have said—even though no one believes you—you have said you don't know who the whistleblower is. So how is this outing the whistleblower?"*

After an ominous pause, Schiff indicated that Jim's time was running out, and he should get back to his questions, but not about the identity of the whistleblower.

There you have the crux of the problem. Adam Schiff, though he had said many a time that he did not know who the whistleblower was—which most everyone believed he did—knew exactly when to pipe up and save a witness from revealing who the whistleblower may be. I think by this time we all knew Adam Schiff was a fact witness in the issue pretending to just be a chairman in search of the truth. His problem was that no one believed that, even if they desperately wanted to believe that the president had done something wrong.

As the hearings continued, the testimony was simply a regurgitation of what had been said behind closed doors in order to try and paint a picture of a president who had put his own ambitions ahead of the country and, in turn, committed an act so egregious that he should no longer be president, or should not be reelected if he was not to be impeached. They could just not let it go. Persistence is one thing, but the continued pursuit of this president was not in the best interest of the country. Yet we continued.

Chairman Schiff finally closed out his show hearings, and in the end, we knew what we knew in the beginning. There was a phone call that some found objectionable and decided that the president should be punished. In the testimony, we found that Gordon Sondland assumed that the aid was being held up for political reasons, although he kept no notes or records and even stated that the president had said there was to be no quid pro quo. We saw a lieutenant colonel testify that he felt the president did not act properly. But when asked if it was ever okay to ask a foreign government to investigate corruption, he said that it would be proper. That leads us to something that should be pointed out. In all the testimony given, it was interesting how one thing rang true with every witness: Ukraine was a corrupt place and corruption was found at all levels of government. In fact, from the transcripts released of the testimony given from witnesses, the corruption in Ukraine was mentioned 820 times. It was found that every witness who was asked about the corruption said that it was pervasive, and many of them agreed with President Trump's assessment of the situation in Ukraine. The corruption was, and for the most part still is, widespread and inherent in the government. It is important to understand this agreed-upon fact when considering why the president may have asked about it, even if it did include a former American vice president and his son. The president has the ultimate responsibility for ensuring that the money that we send overseas is used in the way it was intended and not for corrupt purposes. No matter whether or not you agreed with how President Trump may have carried out his job, this seems to me to be the forgotten part of this whole story. The Democrats would never give him the benefit of the doubt that he was doing his job. They had the optic that they thought would let them get to him, and they would not let anything, even the truth, stand in the way. So as the clock and calendar weighed heavily on the Democrats, they knew that they had to get the report out of the Intel Committee and start the process to complete their impeachment quest.

CHAPTER 6:
THE JUDICIARY COMMITTEE RUBBER-STAMPS INTEL REPORT

The final act was now drawing near. The Judiciary Committee was going to get the report from the Intel Committee and conduct what should be a vigorous and thorough reviewing of the facts and the intense questioning of witnesses, both new and old, which would begin to show whether Congress should go about the business of impeaching Donald Trump. If we were in the real world and not the alternate universe of Democrats hell-bent on finishing a task, you may have seen this process play out. However, since a fair hearing was never the plan, we got a watered-down farce instead that was an embarrassment to not only the House of Representatives but also the Judiciary Committee, and that blame falls at the feet of Chairman Nadler and his members. We on the committee had been left out of the process because of their inept ability to run a committee. And as such, we were playing finisher to the Intel power grab and the railroading of the president. During the time of the Intel hearings, my staff and I worried about the fact that in HR 660 the Democrats were supposed to lay out the rules for how we would handle the proceedings and how the White House would be able to participate. I sent five letters to the chairman asking that he show us what the plans were for when the impeachment tour came to the Judiciary Committee again. Each time, our letters were met with a resounding thud! The silence from the chairman was deafening. We had no idea what to expect, but we knew it would probably be quick and rushed, and provide nothing more than a rubber stamp to the work the Intel Committee had done. We were not disappointed.

It was as bad as we thought. So when the chairman announced that the first hearing would be on December 4, we knew that the time was upon us. The interesting thing is that he said this hearing would be one in which we would look at the historical and constitutional basis for impeachment, as well as the intent of terms such as "high crimes and misdemeanors" for which a president can be removed. I knew right away that this was nothing more than a sham hearing to build support for an impeachment that had no merit. I also came to realize that the hearing would be with law school professors lecturing us about the meaning of impeachment and its basis. I could hardly wait. We knew that the Democrats would line up true believers in the impeachment of Donald Trump, and our expectations were met. So, for my witness, I chose Jonathan Turley. Professor Turley did not vote for President Trump and had been critical of him in many areas, but he did not think that this impeachment was proper, and we needed someone to help us make that case.

Hearings are always a dance between the majority, who controls them, and the minority, who must make the best of what they are given. As this hearing with law school professors drew to a close, I felt that if the Democrats were concerned with at least the appearance of fairness, they would allow us more than one witness. It was not just that I felt it was needed, but it was also the precedent it would set. In the Clinton hearings, they used several outside experts and law professors to lay the legal framework for impeachment. In this case, since we were rushed, and they were not sure what to do anyway, they threw this hearing together on the fly to show we were working. Remember, we just had received the report from the Intel Committee's work the day before. We had not had time to dive into it, but we were going to start the impeachment hearings come hell or high water. As usual, when it came to the willingness of the majority to show a modicum of fairness, they turned and ran the other way. This time, it was rather amusing talking to the chairman about our request.

The lengths that the majority would go to keep this impeachment on track was amazing. I called Chairman Nadler to request one simple thing: that we be granted another witness at the hearing that was scheduled for December 4, 2019. I thought with something this important it would be a simple way for us to get another voice discussing the issue in our favor but also a simple way for the Democrats to show some civility and openness to being fair. They would always have more witnesses than we would, but at least they could give us more than one even, if they in turn increased their number, I offered. When I made the request to the chairman, he got silent for a moment and said he could not do that. I asked him why, and his response was that it was too late. The truth was we still had two days before the hearing, and nothing was set in stone. We still did not even have the report from the Intel hearings. I continued pushing, trying my best to convince him that if he wanted to be taken seriously, he had to at least show he was trying. He just kept repeating that he could not do it and said there was nothing more for us to talk about. I remember this call because I was outside my home in Georgia walking my dog as I was talking to him. It became so ridiculous at one point I looked down at my dog, Cree, and thought I would probably have done better trying to make her understand than I was with my chairman. In the end, Chairman Nadler got so annoyed with me that he hung up on me. I was standing outside of my house with my phone to my ear when he said I am done with this and hung up.

At the time I did not know it, but that call was the perfect analogy for what we were going through in these hearings. The Democrats were so focused on making the deadline that they would not even see when something would have been in their own best interest. Instead, they chose the path of unfairness and manipulation, ensuring that we on the Republican side would continue to show how unfair and partisan this impeachment really was turning out to be. As the darkness and silence overtook me, I just shook my head and realized that the next few weeks were going to be hard and the Democrats were looking at the clock and panicking.

The morning of December 4, 2019, started as they all did for me in Washington, in the gym on the treadmill. It was surreal that morning as I ran and listened to my music and watched the TV screens flash pictures of the hearing room and pictures of Jerry Nadler and me as the day was finally upon us and the House Judiciary Committee was back in the spotlight with the impeachment of Donald Trump. This morning did have a little different feel. Though I have never pitched a no-hitter or bowled a perfect game, I have read stories from people who have. As the end got closer and it appeared the rarity—the no-hitter or the perfect game—might actually happen, those around them would not talk to them or sit close in order not to jinx the moment. Well, that morning it was the same with the Democrats; majority members I saw every morning would not engage in the normal conversations we had most every day. Republicans not on the Judiciary Committee I saw in the gym and in the halls before the hearing came up to me and offered advice or encouragement but did not linger, almost as if saying, *We are not sure what is going to happen today, but we are glad you are there and not us.*

Everything about the day had more of a performance feel than anything else. The first difference was that we had to leave our normal committee room and have the hearing in the Ways and Means Committee room, where the Intel hearings had been conducted. I guess the Judiciary Committee could not be outdone, so we moved to keep the atmosphere going and show these hearings were a big deal. We inquired as to why we were moving and were told it had to do with accommodation for the press and crowd. In the end, we could have gotten along fine in our normal hearing room, but when the optics are the most important part of your case, you must show it off. The Ways and Means room itself is old Washington. It has ceilings that reach up two floors, with ornate decorations all around the walls. It has been the scene of many important hearings over the years, and this was to be no different. In my opinion, however, though it is an impressive room and the optics are tailor-made for congressional hearings from a TV perspective, it is not particularly good for much else. The acoustics are poor when the room is crowded, and the chairs are particularly uncomfortable for the members. I would have thought that a committee as powerful as the Ways and Means Committee would have better chairs for its members. So, for the next few weeks of long hearings, not only would I have to endure the prodding of the Democrats, but I'd also have a chair with springs that kept poking me, making sitting for long periods an even more torturous task. But hey as I had said since January 2019, the show must go on because the Democrats had a promise to keep, and they were going to make it happen.

The hearing was supposed to be about the legal and constitutional foundations of impeachment. In other words, we were inviting law school professors to come and lecture on their opinions about historical impeachment and give their opinions on the current situation. The hearing had three Democrat witnesses, who all had made up their minds about President Trump and the impeachment long before they got there. They were Noah Feldman from Harvard, Pamela Karlan from Stanford, and Michael Gerhardt from the University of North Carolina. The only witness that we were given was Jonathan Turley. As stated earlier, he was not a fan of the president, but he held the view that this was not an impeachable offense and was willing to discuss the progression or, in my view, the decline in the standards for impeachment. If we had gotten the second witness, we would have called Alan Dershowitz, who eventually did serve on the president's legal team during the Senate trial. But thanks to the unwillingness of Jerry Nadler, we only had one witness. At the end of this first hearing, it was apparent to all that we only needed one.

The energy level in the room was high as it got closer to our start time of 10 a.m. Reporters were everywhere, along with video and still cameras. Whenever a member walked in, it was a frenzy of sound as the photographers snapped away, documenting the lead-up to the hearing. When Chairman Nadler gaveled the proceedings in and gave his opening statement, you could tell that these proceedings were all a sham to get to a preordained date with impeachment. The main point we wanted to get across was to emphasize the unfairness of the process and how the Democrats were willing to go to any length, including changing or ignoring the rules, to get their intended results. We would start the day by pointing that out.

After my opening statement for the hearing, I made a motion under the rules that we as a committee call Adam Schiff as a witness. The Democrats, of course, shut the motion and debate down by having

Congresswoman Zoe Lofgren (D-CA) make a motion to table, essentially killing the motion. We had just gotten the report from the Intel Committee the day before the hearing started. We had every right to want to hear from the author of the report and would make the Democrats deal with that every chance we could. The willingness to table the request instead of deal with it revealed more and more evidence of the shoddy and unprofessional way these proceedings were being carried out. We knew that they did not have anything that would rise to the level of impeachment. But they were in the majority. We in the minority would remind the American people over and over that this was a sham impeachment in which facts did not matter.

I also continued to emphasize in my remarks that the chairman of the committee, Jerry Nadler, in the Clinton impeachment was the one making the best arguments against what was happening to us now—namely, we were not allowed to participate and the whole process was rushed and did a disservice to the American people and our legislative body. Using the Democrats' own words against them was the best way to make our point that the process had devolved into nothing more than a partisan pursuit born out of dislike of President Trump.

The hearing that I dubbed the law professor hearing yielded nothing that we did not know except an in-depth discussion of the history of bribery and impeachment. The witnesses went according to script. Noah Feldman stated that he felt that the call alone between President Trump and President Zelensky was enough to impeach the president. Michael Gerhardt exclaimed that if this was not impeachable, then nothing was impeachable. Pamela Karlan agreed with that assessment, saying that the evidence was so damning that it struck at the very heart of who we are as a nation. The Democrat witnesses all agreed that Congress, for the good of our democracy, must continue on this path of impeachment.

Our witness, Jonathan Turley, presented a different perspective and one that put the Democrats on their heels. In fact, most of the Democratic members did not engage Mr. Turley at all. Mr. Turley's comments went right to the heart of what we had been saying from the beginning—that the evidence shown so far was nowhere close to what the standard of impeachment ought to be. He stated, "To impeach a President on this record would expose every future president to the same type of inchoate impeachment." He went on to hit the motive that I have expressed often about the motive to get the president outweighed the evidence when he said, "Principle often takes us to a place where we would prefer not to be." It was of little use to say this to the Democrats on the Judiciary Committee they had tunnel vision when it came to this president the entire year. One of the most lasting and biting comments that came from Jonathan Turley that day, however, was one that was directed back at Congress, specifically the Democrat majority. He stated that if they proceeded with obstruction of Congress charges against this president after Congress had failed to avail itself of the necessary remedies available to it to get information from the administration, then there would be obstruction, but it would be obstruction by Congress!

The hearing was another stall and waste of time for the Judiciary Committee, but it did allow for some interesting moments. I have watched people in politics lose arguments when they get what my first Speaker of the House in Georgia described as being too cute by half. Well early in the hearing Professor Karlan found out what that meant when she tried to be snarky, and it backfired. During questioning from Shelia Jackson Lee (D-TX), Professor Karlan was asked, "What comparisons can we make between kings, that the framers were afraid of, and the president's conduct today?" This was during a discussion about the history of impeachment and its working under British law and the monarchy. It was an otherwise painfully boring part of the hearing, which had settled into a slow lull of monotony. The question sought to show that unlike the monarchy in England, the president was not a king. Professor Karlan chose to take this question beyond expounding on the fact that the king's word was the law, while here in the US, that is not true. She said the president cannot use Article Two of our Constitution to do whatever he wanted to do. Instead of making her point, the professor chose to extend the discussion with an analogy that showed her animus toward the president and her desire to see him impeached. Noting that in the Constitution, there are no titles of nobility, she went on to say, "While the president can name his son Barron, he can't make him a baron." The joke fell as flat as the professor's credibility. Another example of being too cute by half and losing your point to hubris.

The president, who was on his way to NATO meetings, was watching the hearings, and White House officials who were with us in the hearing room reported that he was furious. He had already lashed out because the hearings were being conducted while he was out of the country, and this just added insult to injury. There were many areas that the Democrats could have ventured into, but attacking the thirteen-year-old son of the president just showed the determined folly of their actions. I told them the Trump officials would respond, and we did. Matt Gaetz (R-FL) got into a very heated discussion with the professor, who later apologized for her words. Matt summed it up best when he told the professor that her comments were inappropriate and, in the end, only served to make her look mean. The First Lady nailed it when she tweeted: "A minor child deserves privacy and should be kept out of politics. Pamela Karlan, you should be ashamed of your very angry and obviously biased public pandering, and using a child to do it." Congressman Mike Johnson (R-LA) later read the First Lady's comment into the *Congressional Record* so that it would be a part of the official record.

At the end of the day, the words of Jonathan Turley spoke loudly when he said that the impeachment had a very thin record and that, if anything, if Congress proceeded on the charge of obstruction, it was Congress that would be guilty of obstruction. Yet, as the saying goes, the show must go on, and even with bad reviews and little to nothing accomplished, Chairman Nadler pushed on by saying that all three parts of impeachment had been met: he president requested that the Ukraine investigate Biden, the witness testimony at the hearing that said it was high crimes and misdemeanors, and the biggest whopper of them all that the majority of the American people were supportive of impeachment. I guess when you have nothing, the best offense is to keep saying things you hope to be true long enough that someone believes that they are. If this was supposed to be a true investigation, in search of facts, it was a failure so far, and it would only get worse.

Chairman Nadler had allowed the Judiciary Committee to become a rubber stamp without even the perception of fairness and respectability. We were simply the hand maidens of the Intel Committee and Adam Schiff. The next hearings that were scheduled would not get us any closer to the truth because instead of talking to fact witnesses, or even Adam Schiff himself, we would have staff question staff in the ultimate vanity exercise rolled out by the Democrats to make their high-powered outside counsel feel like their year of help had not been entirely wasted. However, before we could even move the charade down the line, the Speaker who saw the clock and realized that time was running out chose to weigh in and the end was finally acknowledged. In the next twenty-four hours, the charade was revealed, and the final countdown was on.

I have always contended that the reason the Intel Committee was brought in to do the hearings for the impeachment was that it was never set up for contentious public hearings and its members were not used to the down-and-dirty process fights that happened in other committees, and especially the Judiciary Committee. I remember a member once coming up to me after a particularly ugly Judiciary hearing and shaking his head and saying, "There is no way I would ever be on that committee. Y'all not only fight all the time, but you seem to enjoy it." Well, to a certain extent, my friend was right. We viewed the committee as the keeper of the standard for debate and process in the House. If the Judiciary Committee could not be a place for rowdy, raucous debates over issues, all while staying within the bounds of proper committee decorum, then where else was it going to happen? The House floor is a scripted dance with each person getting their minutes in to show the folks back home that they have an opinion on a particular issue. Unfortunately, real debate rarely occurs on the floor, so the only place left is the committee rooms. So, after a year of the Judiciary Democrats looking like the gang that could not get its act together, the move to Intel was not surprising.

What was interesting to me was what happened when it came back to Judiciary, as we all knew it would. Adam Schiff was not there to control the proceedings, and we on the Republican side were ready to do what we do best: fight for the causes we believe in. This cause was easy in our minds. The Democrats were overreaching, and it wasn't just that they were factually wrong. They were abusing the process to accomplish it. So, when we got the ball back, we made sure that, at every opportunity, we would point out the deficiencies of not only process but also facts. The obvious point from round one with the law school professors was that the Democrats brought forward partisan individuals who did not give the appearance of being open-minded or presenting facts that let people make up their minds for themselves. And when you had gaffes like the hit on the president's son, I could just imagine the Speaker and her staff having flashbacks to the bucket of chicken and the early circus found in the Judiciary. I am sure that it was with the hearing fresh in her mind that the Speaker of the House decided to remove all doubt. And without any more hearings needed, although we would have one just to say we did, it was time to draft articles of impeachment. Speaker Pelosi held a press conference, and as she had done so many times in this process, just declared that the process had revealed enough, that the president was guilty, and that it was time to write the articles.

Speaker Pelosi was reported in *Politico* to have said, "The president leaves us no choice but to act because he is trying to corrupt, once again, the election for his own benefit." It is funny to me that even during this investigation into a call with a foreign leader by the president she reached back to the old lie that he interfered in the previous election, refuted by the Mueller report. She just could never bring herself to admit that Hillary Clinton was just a bad candidate who could not relate to the American people. Her other comment just made my eyes roll: "Sadly, but with confidence and humility, with allegiance to our founders and our heart full of love for our America, today I am asking our chairmen to proceed with articles of impeachment."

The blatant disrespect that had been going on for the rules of the House, and the determination that the president was assumed guilty and that he had to prove his innocence, meant that her remarks, which she wrapped in patriotic rhetoric, showed her disdain for the president and, in my opinion, the institution she led. The one good thing that we knew was there was no more false posturing by the Democrats needed; they could now just admit that they were going to impeach the president without having to pretend anymore.

The chairman announced that the hearing for the following week would be on the report issued by the Intel Committee. This would lead to one of the strangest hearings I was ever a part of and probably one of the strangest ever in Congress, and that is saying something. In this hearing, we would hear from no fact witnesses, just staff from the committees. We will get to this fiasco in a bit, but in the meantime, we had to figure out how to handle the hearings because the first part of the hearing was going to be a presentation on impeachment by the staffs of the Intel Committee and the Judiciary Committee. It should be noted that we had no input into the Intel Committee's work, and the Judiciary Committee had not conducted our own inquiry, so we were completely in the dark as to how we would respond to a work product from the Judiciary *that did not exist.* The problem we had was, with our limited staff, how do we respond to a report we did not write and was not involved with? Additionally, we would have to guess what the Democrats' argument would be for a Judiciary perspective on the impeachment elements. After spending time with our staff and the staffs of the other committees that had been working on the hearings within the Intel Committee, we decided that our effort would be led by Stephen Castor, who had been working the investigation as the lead Republican counsel on the House Oversight Committee. Stephen has been on the Hill for a while and was familiar with the contentious nature of what we were going through—not just now but through battles with the IRS, Benghazi, and the Fast and Furious investigations. He was knowledgeable and articulate.

I know that many outside Washington do not think much of the staff members who help us in our offices and on our committees, but I will tell you that I was blessed with great staff help during this time, and the impeachment proceedings showcased the talent of these great individuals who had chosen to work on the Hill, often turning down much more lucrative opportunities in the private market. It was also a chance for me to highlight the difference in how we viewed the staff we worked with as contrasted with the Democrats.

In stark contrast to our approach of using in-house staff, Chairman Nadler and Chairman Schiff reached outside their own staffs and brought in hired guns to do the work for them. Barry Berke and Norm Eisen in the Judiciary Committee and Daniel Goldman for the Intel Committee were all brought in with what appeared to be the express purpose of taking down President Trump. These three attorneys are very good at what they do, and their collective legal skills are impressive, as is their commitment to the Democratic Party. If I were to deal with them in a courtroom setting, I could see how their skills would be useful, and to an extent, that played out here in the committee. But most of the time, their presentation just came off as heavy-handed. It also appeared that they were pushing for their own spotlight more than the committee that hired them. They will come up more in the hearings that lie just ahead, but it should be noted that the difference in approach and style was obvious. We did battle with whom we had; the Democrats did not trust their staff, so they went out and brought in help. I expressed this sentiment to the chairman and his staff then, and I say it now. The staff attorneys on the Democrat side of the committee who showed up every day and worked on all the issues before the committee were very good attorneys. I may have disagreed with them on most things, but they were dedicated public servants who did everything, not just the glamorous stuff. It would have been interesting to see what those Democrat staff members could have done. But instead, as Barry and Norm were playing their part before the camera, my lead investigative counsel, Ashley Callen, who helped put our case together, was sitting in the spot next to me. During a presentation by Barry Berke, Norm was sitting next to Chairman Nadler during the testimony. Nothing was wrong with that except I believe the Democrats did not like the optics. So, they put one of their very capable female staff next to Chairman Nadler at a break. They did not let her do anything but rather used her for the optics. More than once I asked Nadler, "Why do you not use your own staff?" But Nadler would just typically look away and mumble.

I could see that even if the staff would never say it, the slight to them was a real slap at their daily contribution to the Democrats' work on the committee. It is very analogous to the Democrats' case. They preferred the show to the substance, and with that, we moved deeper into the sham show.

As we headed into the next hearing, we knew that what was what. Pelosi had decreed that she had heard enough and that the articles should be drafted. She could not even give Chairman Nadler the cover of having a final hearing that could have at least have been spun as an attempt to fair and impartial. According to the Speaker, it was time to move forward with the impeachment because time was running out. The hearing that was scheduled was for the presentation of the Intel Committee report and a report from the Democrats on the Judiciary Committee on what they judged to be the impeachable offenses committed by Donald Trump. The hearing was a farce from the beginning, with even reporters asking why we were going through with it, given that there were no new details and that Pelosi had already weighed in on the matter.

Before the hearing was called to order that morning, we were treated to one of the more memorable moments of the impeachment charade. Stephen Castor, our Republican counsel, came into what would probably be the most high-profile appearance of his life carrying a reusable Whole Foods bag. He had a lot of stuff, and without thinking about the massive amount of attention he would attract at the hearing, he picked up the bag, filled it up, and came to the hearing. We laughed about it before he went out to the hearing room, but we had no idea that within the next few minutes it would go viral on Twitter. It was a wonderful moment that reflected the kind of person Stephen is. He is a hard worker who cares more about substance than appearance. I wish I could have convinced the Democrats that this was a virtue.

The hearing from a format standpoint is what will go down in history as strange. Here is the procedure that we followed that day. The staff counsel for the Republicans and Democrats on the House Judiciary Committee each had one hour to give opening statements; from there, Republican and Democratic counsel from the House Intelligence

Committee had an hour and a half to present evidence. After all this had been presented, the staff counsel from the Intelligence Committee would spend the rest of the hearings taking questions from lawmakers. In my wildest dreams, I could not think of a better way to waste a Monday, and believe me, I tried!

The way the hearing was set up was bad enough, but with Pelosi's announcement that they should already be drafting impeachment articles, it took away what could have been any interest in the hearing. Jerry Nadler had hoped for one more grand display of supposed evidence, which he would then use to announce there was enough to impeach. Instead, we got a hearing that was a waste of time and only fueled the vanity of the hired-hand counsels from the Democrat Intel and Judiciary Committees. This was on display from the start. Barry Berke, counsel for the Democrats on the Judiciary Committee, led off and gave the presentation that the president should be removed, and then Stephen Castor gave the Republicans' perspective. It then moved to one of the real movers in this investigation, Daniel Goldman. He was the counsel for the Intel Committee Democrats. It was Mr. Goldman who had worked with Adam Schiff to arrange the previous two months of witnesses and investigations. He was not a fan of the president, and it showed.

The tragedy of these hearings was that we never could get Adam Schiff to testify. If you listened to him, he would let you know on any interview that he was in charge and that the evidence showed the president was guilty. Yet, when it came time to defend with actual results, Adam punted and was nowhere to be found. He knew that if he presented the report, he would have to answer questions. Adam Schiff's actions showed, just like his report, that he would rather make vague accusations than sit for a true discussion about what was being done. It became the steady drumbeat of our side. Where is Adam? I guess it is much easier to talk about things when you do not have to answer questions. An interesting note for history here. The man whose office (and more than likely the man himself) had contact with the whistleblower, who oversaw developing the case against President Trump and masterminding the impeachment plan, never had to stand

and answer a single question about his actions and what he put our country through. In fact, as it turned out, Congressman Jamie Raskin (D-MD) and I were the only members who gave testimony as to what was happening, when we testified for over eight hours later at the House Rules Committee before the articles of impeachment went to the floor. He was incredibly good at using others to do his work for him. That may have been good for Adam Schiff but not so much for Daniel Goldman. Mr. Goldman was in for a long day, especially after Mr. Berke decided to abuse his position and go after Mr. Castor. I was not going to let that happen.

The main thing to understand about these hearings was not what was said but what can you get the media or social media to pick up on and help spread. For the Democrats they were trying to get out through the morass of reports that somehow Donald Trump had done something so bad that he should be impeached. They knew that the Senate would never vote to remove him, so the next best thing was to damage him enough that he could not win the next election. This was their game plan, but given they did not have time on their side, they also had to bend the process to make the show seem fair when it most certainly was not. In my mind, we needed to focus only on two points. First, nothing in the call or the actions surrounding the call was wrong, and even if somehow you thought otherwise, the actions were nowhere near close to the standard for impeachment. Second, the inherent unfairness in the process made the Democrats look like bitter party hacks only out to destroy a political enemy. Many in the country were starting to see that.

The plan was to use this hearing to put the evidence out there and then move on to the articles that were ordered by Pelosi, but somewhere along the way to a smooth exit they forgot that the high-powered attorneys they brought in had to have their day in the sun. The first was Barry Berke. On this day if he had just given the Judiciary presentation and then left the stage most would have forgotten his appearance. The problem came when after he gave his thirty-minute presentation he sat down beside the chairman. I thought to myself surely this was just to waste some time and when it came time for questioning, he would surely yield to a Democratic staff attorney or to his associate Norm Eisen. That did not happen, and he stayed in the chair to handle part of the forty-five-minute question time that was allowed under the rules. This elicited more than a few concerns from our side. You told us we had to be happy with staff testifying about the report and not Adam Schiff, but now you are saying that Mr. Berke could be a witness and a prosecutor in the same day? That was just too much for most of us to take and what could have been a boring hearing became a fight because the Democrats did not care about the appearance—they just wanted to take their pound of flesh.

When Mr. Berke started interrogating Mr. Castor while he was in the witness chair it turned ugly. It would have been one thing to ask his side questions to elaborate their story but when he started to attack Steve, our side started to act out and called for the chairman to reign this interrogation in. Jim Sensenbrenner (R-WI) piped up by saying Mr. Berke was badgering the witness, and many on our side starting lodging protests, which the chairman just ignored and started loudly banging the gavel as our voices got louder. The funny thing was the more Chairman Nadler got frustrated that we would not let up, the louder he banged. At one point during my protest to him, during which he just kept banging the gavel louder and louder, I said to him, "Bang it harder, still does not make what is going on right." Finally, the forty-five minutes of interrogation by Mr. Berke ended, and I was furious. All throughout our prep for the hearing with the members, I and others encouraged our members to stay away from Mr. Goldman, a particularly good partisan attorney who had been feeding the narrative behind the scenes with Chairman Schiff for a long time. Make no mistake, he is a true believer in the Democratic cause and was there for a reason. The problem Mr. Goldman had was that after his colleague went after Mr. Castor as unfairly as he did, I did not care anymore and determined that I would go after him.

When it came time for me to ask questions, I was fit to be tied. The disrespect that had been shown by Mr. Berke and the chairman toward Mr. Castor was an offense that would lead to what would become one of the more memorable exchanges of the hearing. The notable exchange lasted about twelve minutes as I questioned him about two areas: the actions of Joe Biden in Ukraine, when in a story related later by the former vice president, he admitted to demanding a quid pro quo from the Ukrainian leadership, and the inclusion of the numbers of Ranking Member Devin Nunes, Rudy Giuliani, and members of the press in the Schiff report, which was completely inappropriate. The following is a transcript of the interaction that I had with Daniel Goldman at the hearing. In it you sense the tension in the room, and if you watch the video you can see that Mr. Goldman, who enjoys asking questions, does not like to be held accountable.

Doug Collins: And you are not going to hear anything from me about a subpoena. And the legality of a subpoena. My problem is this. Who on the committee asked that those numbers that you actually did put into for subpoena and get those numbers back? Who was it that asked that they be crosschecked for members of the media and members of Congress? Who ordered that?

Daniel Goldman: I don't think that's how we did it, sir.

Doug Collins: No. Whoa, Whoa, Whoa. You came out with a report that actually showed these people, such as Chairman Nunes and others, were actually on these calls.

Daniel Goldman: Yes.

Doug Collins: Now, someone…and, you and I, we're not going to play cute here. Somebody took the four records that you asked for, the at least four. Took those numbers and then said, hey, let's play match game. Who ordered the match game for members of Congress and the press? Was it you?

Daniel Goldman: I don't think anyone did, sir.

Doug Collins: Then how did you get…okay, come on, that's the most ridiculous item I've ever heard. You don't just all of a sudden pick-up numbers in which you have to match those numbers to actually show where they are and you don't come up with them. Who ordered them to actually match for members of Congress and the press?

Daniel Goldman: That's actually…what you just described is exactly how it happens.

Doug Collins: Who ordered you to find out if Nunes's number was on those calls?

Daniel Goldman: If I could just explain, sir. You pick an event of significance in the investigation and you look for sequencing and patterns surrounding that event. You look then at the numbers and you try to identify what those numbers are. And, then, you start to build the circumstantial case.

Doug Collins: At this point. That's a wonderful explanation, but not an answer to my question. Those are you looking for the four numbers you asked for and to see how they're connected. I understand the subpoena that you issued. My question directly, was it you or was it chairman Schiff that said, "While we're doing this, let's see if this matches chairman Nunes's number? Let's see if this matches a member of the press' number." Somebody along the way just didn't all of a sudden having an epiphany, unless you're getting ready to throw a low level staffer under the bus, that these numbers might match. So, who did it? Was it chairman Schiff or was it you. Be careful. You're under oath.

Daniel Goldman: I know I'm under oath, sir. It doesn't matter.

Doug Collins: Then answer the question.

Daniel Goldman: And I will answer the question if you'll give me a second here. It's not a simple answer.

Doug Collins: The same second that was not afforded in my witness, by the way.

Daniel Goldman: Well, I think he was allowed to answer the question.

Doug Collins: Who decided to leak it, by the way? If you're not going to tell me the other story. While you're thinking about how you're going to answer that question, who decided to leak it? The information. Why did you include it in the report?

Daniel Goldman: That's not a leak, sir.

Doug Collins: How did you include it in the report? After not saying anything else about this, not publicly known. So, two questions are hanging out that everybody's looking for an answer for, including me. Who ordered it? Was it you or was it chairman Schiff? And, then, why was it decided, except for nothing but smear purposes, to be included in the Schiff report?

Daniel Goldman: Well, I'm not going to get into the deliberations of our investigation with you. And, I will tell you the reason it was included in the report is because the calls were a surrounding important evidence to our investigation. And, I think that your question is, frankly, not better directed...not at me, but at the people who were having conversations.

Doug Collins: Oh no, no, no. We're not going to play that game.

Daniel Goldman: The people involved in the president's scheme.

Doug Collins: We're not going to play that game. You're as good as Mr. Burke. You're not going to play that game. You're not answering a question. And, every member of the media, everybody here, when you start going into the decorum of this House, when you start looking at members' telephone numbers, you start looking in reporters' telephone numbers, which, they ought to be scared about. You took a subpoena for four. And, then, you decided to play match game. You found numbers that you thought were...some of them actually didn't exist. Because, they claimed that they were for the White House budget office, and, they were not. So, we're throwing stories out there because nobody was—

Daniel Goldman: That's not true.

Doug Collins: Nobody was out there action. So, I go back to my question. Are you going to go on record, in front of everybody here today, and say that you will not tell who ordered this? You, or, Mr. Gold...Mr. Goldman, you, or Mr. Schiff?

Daniel Goldman: I am going to go on record and tell you that I'm not going to reveal how we conducted this investigation.

Doug Collins: And, that's the problem we have with this entire thing. Mr. Schiff said behind closed doors the entire time.

Daniel Goldman: I can tell you what the importance is—

Doug Collins: I'm done with you for right now. We're done. You're not answering the question. You're not being honest about this answer because you know who it is. You're just not answering.

When I turned the questioning over to Ashley, I was more convinced than ever that this sham was in and of itself an attack on the American people as much as it was an attack on President Trump. The rest of the hearing dragged on throughout the day and at the end left nothing but hard feelings and nothing new. It was so bad that by the time we ended, most of the spectators had gone home and the reporters were glassy-eyed, longing to be anywhere else. We had done our job, and I was proud of our members. They had risen to the task, stayed focused, and presented the case to the world that this was a sham in the making. I also take great comfort in the performance of my counsel, Ashley Callen, and of Stephen Castor who did yeoman's duty. They showed that no matter what some may say, many of the people who work on the Hill are good folks just trying to do a good job no matter what that job is. They are there day in and day out, not just for the exciting stuff. So, when Stephen packed up his Whole Foods bag for the night, he walked out of that hearing room tired but with his head held high. The fight was not finished, but the charade was exposed and the only thing for the Democrats to do was bring the articles of impeachment and let the sham play itself out.

The one thing that had bothered me about this impeachment was that it was not coming from, in my mind, a principled place. It was not being brought after exhaustive investigation that found the commission of an actual crime. No, it was being brought because the Democrats thought they had the right mix of circumstances to be able to sell an impeachment that did not show an impeachable offense. This became obvious because while we were involved in these proceedings it was leaked that the Democratic Party had done focus groups based on how to sell these allegations to the American people. Instead of letting the supposed wrong deeds speak for themselves, they went shopping for the right words that would help convince the American people that they were right. The change came in how they talked about certain things;

for example, the term "quid pro quo" was changed to "bribery" or another bad-sounding word like "extortion." This change came about because the Democratic Congressional Campaign Committee (DCCC) conducted a focus groups to test their messaging. I knew the Democrats were having trouble with the impeachment, but I would have never thought they would have paid people to tell them which words played better when talking about impeachment. The way they went about this showed this was not about principled investigation; it was about getting the president at all costs. In other words, they thought the average person was too dumb to understand what was going on, so they would dumb it down for them. The contempt for the American people by the Democrats never ceases to amaze me.

When Rep. Jim Himes (D-CT) appeared on NBC's *Meet the Press*, Chuck Todd asked him why the Democrats had stopped using the term "quid pro quo." Himes replied, "Number one, when you're trying to try to persuade the American people of something that is really pretty simple…it's probably best not to use Latin words to explain it…. We've got to get off this 'quid pro quo' thing because it's complicated."

Again, they belittle the American people as not being as smart and as sophisticated as them. It was this kind of arrogance that let me know that no matter how hard they tried they would not be able to pull this off. I have watched when people from all sides have taken the voters for granted, and every time the voters are in on the joke and it seems to always backfire. The old saying that the truth is as good as a lie would fit in this case except for the fact that the truth was against the Democrats, so they had to walk with the lie.

Far be it from the Democrats to try and actually find and make a case against the president. Instead as I said many times, in these hearings this was a focus-group impeachment. They never had the facts, so they chose cheap tricks, innuendo, and falsehoods to draft articles of impeachment. The sad chapter was playing itself out to its forgone conclusion, but before we could get to finalizing impeachment, we had to tear down a world leader and continue to try and make the world believe that the acts involved in a phone call were worthy of impeachment. It was truly a sad time.

In two days, the articles were finished, and Chairman Nadler rushed to get our markup scheduled so we could get the articles passed out of the committee and on to the floor before the Christmas break. Now if you are keeping time, we had been at this less than a week. We had two hearings that were nothing but political theater. We had heard from no fact witnesses or outside witnesses, and we had not even heard from the leader of the committee who wrote the report they were basing the impeachment on. The speed of these proceedings showed that the Democrats were not interested in anything except getting the articles done and out of the Judiciary Committee as soon as possible. They knew the process was rushed and looked bad, but they had to get though the markup of these articles, and it would be a painfully long day.

When the day arrived, it was a special time for me. It was the holiday season, and the White House Christmas party for Congress was scheduled for that week. The reason it was special was that my wife, Lisa, was in town. I had promised that I would take her to the party. She rarely gets to come to Washington, and with impeachment going on and a Christmas party at the White House, what a better time for her to visit? So, the week started with promise. But as it dragged on, it turned into what this affair had been from the beginning: an unmitigated disaster and waste of time.

If you do not follow Congress, which I assume most do not on a day-to-day basis, when a bill or resolution is ready to be voted on, it goes through a process called markup, which is where both sides get to debate the bill and offer amendments. Sometimes this can go quickly, but with something as important as this, it was not going to go that way or be smooth. The Democrats had brought only two charges in the impeachment. The first was abuse of power, which was based on the idea that President Trump had abused the authority of his office for personal gain during his phone call with President Zelensky. The second charge was obstruction of Congress. This was based on the president not providing everything the Democrats wanted, even if it was illegal to give. I just remind you, on this obstruction charge, that it was Jonathan Turley who said if the Democrats went forward with this, the only obstruction would be that of Congress.

In the months leading up to this markup of the articles of impeachment, many things were said about the phone call that started this whole process. However, past all the spin from the Democrats, there were some basic problems with the story. Jim Jordan, congressman from Ohio, is a tenacious questioner, and very good at breaking things down into small but memorable sound bites that help deliver the same message over and over again. He had developed what he called the four things that never changed about the phone call. Many of our committee members, including me, adapted our own version of the four truths that never changed for when we talked about the president's call with President Zelensky.

Here are mine:

- Both President Zelensky and President Trump said that there was no pressure on either side during the call. In fact, President Zelensky said publicly that he never felt pressured.

- The transcript of the call clearly showed there was no conditionality placed on the aid and the investigation.

- The Ukrainians were not even aware that the aid was being withheld when the two men spoke.

- The Ukrainians never opened an investigation, and still they received the money that was set out for them ahead of the deadline for when the money was due.

As hard as the Democrats tried, they never could overcome these four basic facts that ran contrary to their entire case. One of the worst situations you can find yourself in is having promised a result but not having the resources to deliver that result. In this case, it was the impeachment of Donald Trump. They had not made the case as many times they tried, and now they were at the end with a very thin evidence trail to convince the world they were right. One of the sad parts of their argument was that to make people believe that there was something nefarious on the call, they had to make you believe that the president of Ukraine was in fear of, or felt intimidated by, President Trump. Much to the Democrats' dismay, this was just not true, and President Zelensky said so on many occasions. So, the way the Democrats combatted this was to say that at best he was afraid to say anything else because his country still needed help and he could not let anything that he thought or believed interfere with them being able to get what they wanted from the United States. So, the first excuse was that he was a frightened coward. As you can tell, this did not go over with most people, but especially our side, where we just kept hammering the Democrats for disparaging another world leader in front of the world and especially his detractors in his own country. It was beneath the dignity of the House, but the Democrats were desperate, and they had no shame. The rhetoric picked up in this hearing when Steve "Chicken Bucket" Cohen described the head of another country being so scared that he was acting like a battered spouse—too scared to go against President Trump for fear of retribution. I was appalled, but when you have no shame, you will say anything to get your point across. There seemed no end to the depths to which the Democrats would stoop, but if your end is to remove or hurt a political opponent, then you believe you are on a righteous path that is worth the price you pay. The problem is I believe some on the Democratic side sold a piece of their own soul with the baseless attack not only on our president but also the president of Ukraine.

The other thing about this final hearing that continued was the theme that we had lived through all year, which was the blatant disregard for the rules of the House and the committee or, for that matter, even the rules that we had just recently passed in HR 660, which laid out but never really defined the rules for the proceedings. In the last hearing, Rep. Mike Johnson (R-LA) asked what rules we were to follow when it came to objecting to what a witness said. Chairman Nadler replied that we would use the rules of the committee and the House. When we pushed harder for clarification, you could see the frustration building with our members. We were being told by the Democrats that we would follow the rules, but the majority members never defined the rules so we could apply them. Believe me, this train was on the tracks, and it was not about to slow down or try to find its way out of the circular reasoning of the chairman.

As the hearing began, I was sitting next to the chairman when he started to read his opening statement. The majority had decided to start the hearing at 7:00 p.m. on the first evening to get the opening statements and statements of other members out of the way so the next day we could start with amendments. I believe they had another reason: to start in prime time when networks would break in and cover it, thus capturing the nation's attention. Remember, the objective was never to find the truth of the issue at hand; it was to convince the public they had a case. So, in his opening statement I had expected more of the same talking points we had heard before. When he stated that it was with a "heavy heart" that he had to go through with this, I was not sure if I wanted to laugh out loud, cry, or maybe must go to the restroom and vomit. I had seen the entire year that at every hearing that the chairman thought would be a blow to the president he would be in an excited mood. The day of the Mueller hearing you would have thought he had won the lottery. The chairman and his entire committee had been so caught up in a type of tunnel vision that could only see the president being damaged that they let most everything else go to make this happen. For him to say this now was just too much to take. I should have just reminded myself of this one truth: every time the committee thought they had what they were looking for to hurt the president or a group of members and staff typically left the Democrats with long faces and few answers to give to the media on why the day was not as good as they had hoped or promised. Today would be the same. The petty thinking and complete dislike of this president would be on full display, and they would finish the job no matter what.

In the first article of impeachment, which was abuse of power, we continually hit back on the four facts I outlined earlier. It was amazing to me that the Democrat argument, after all the attempts to find something to impeach this president on, came down to their contention that President Trump abused his office for personal gain on a phone call in which the party who was supposedly abused stated on numerous occasions that he never felt pressured or forced to act in any way. The point that I could not believe was that to make their point the Democrats sought to tear down Zelensky and make him seem weak. This was a devasting argument to make against a leader who was at the time in a shooting war with Russia. The lowest point in the hearing came when Steve Cohen went off on a speech about many of the scandals that they thought hurt the president. He mentioned things like Stormy Daniels, Michael Cohen, and past Trump business endeavors, like Trump University. He then went on to say that President Zelensky was not going to say anything bad about President Trump because he had Russia at this door threatening him and that even if he had been pressured, he would have never brought it up. Continuing his attack on President Zelensky, he stated that he was either one of two things, an actor or a just a politician. He was basically saying that the president of a sovereign country, Ukraine, was just a liar because we all know that actors just read what they are given, and that politicians lie. AMAZING. We had turned into a committee committed to not only taking out our own president, but also we were attacking foreign leaders. However, Steve did reveal where he learned his use of drama and props, such as his infamous chicken bucket episode from earlier in the year: he had studied drama in college. How far we had fallen.

Aside from all the bickering and accusations that were being thrown back and forth by both sides, we were there to take up the articles of impeachment. The markup gave us the opportunity to offer amendments that we felt could change the language of the articles to show how misguided they were and another opportunity to use the amendments to make our case about what had been left out by the Democrats in their pursuit of the president. I do not want you to be under any illusion that we thought that by attempting to amend these articles we could arrive at point of somehow agreeing with them. No, you cannot fix what is inherently broken, but we could lay out our case one more time before we went to the floor and vote on sending the articles to the Senate. In the minority, in cases like this, you can't change the outcome, but when it is as wrong as what was happening to our country and to the president of the United States, you could make it as painful as possible.

The first article was the very amorphous charge of abuse of power. The Democrats stated that the president's actions on the call were wrong because he sought personal gain through his official actions. They had always tried to tie the claimed withholding of funds and the promise of a White House meeting as proof that the president was trying to get Zelensky to investigate Joe Biden, which would hurt his presidential campaign. As we had stated all along, for this to be true there must be an actual threat in which President Zelensky felt pressured or threatened into an action. The truth is that he did not, and the funds came—before the statutory deadline—without Zelensky having to do anything. So, you may be asking yourself, *Why would they make such a vague charge against the president?* I am glad you asked.

The real reason for the charge can be traced back to the words of that congressman who was the gift that just keeps on giving: Steve Cohen. The reason was that by using such an open-ended charge the committee and the other members of the Democratic Party could talk about anything they wanted and claim it was an abuse of power, even if the allegations had nothing to do with why the impeachment hearings were called. When Steve Cohen brought up the scandals I mentioned earlier about the president's personal life, his personal attorney, and his business dealings, this was not a mistake. If the Democrats had had an actual crime they could have charged, they would have quicker than anything. They longed to have a valid charge, but as the investigation continued and Speaker Pelosi forced them to write the articles of impeachment, even if they could not find something they could prove, they came up with the brilliant move to charge nothing but at the same time charge everything. This strategy allowed them to give cover to their vulnerable members up for reelection in tough districts. It allowed them to focus-group their districts to see what issues played worst for the president. If it was his private business dealings, then they would use that for the definition of abuse of power if someone did not believe the call itself was improper. They could use immigration, gun control, or even his tweets as a basis for abuse of power if people did not believe their charge as it related to the phone call between President Trump and President Zelensky. I find it interesting to this day that whenever I brought this up and challenged it, the Democrats really did not attack my premise head on. They would skate around it or just say I was covering for the president. Over the next few weeks, though, it became clear to me as I watched Democrats talk about the impeachment and try to lump in anything he did that they did not like as an abuse of power. The sad truth was the only abuse of power was their own.

In dealing with the second charge, obstruction of Congress, the whole argument really revolved around this fact: the president acted like a president and did not give in to the Democrats every time they screamed or wanted something and he did not give it to them or he gave it to them in a way they did not like, they would just say it was obstruction. Chairman Schiff even stated that if a witness did not appear that on its face was obstruction no matter what valid legal reason they had for not appearing. I agreed with Jonathan Turley that if they went through with the obstruction charge, it was really the Democrats who were causing the obstruction. The real problem is that there was such a strict, self-imposed time deadline, the Democrats could not even go through proper procedure to get the information they were looking for.

The impatience of Chairman Nadler was evident all year. In this one year alone, he had issued more subpoenas than his predecessor did in his entire six years as chairman. He would not stoop to engage in negotiations with witnesses in the administration. This was obvious when instead of setting up a plan to have Attorney General Barr testify in our committee, Chairman Nadler stuck to his position that it would be under these new rules for staff questioning to continue the illusion of a formal impeachment-style investigation. Chairman Schiff of the Intel Committee and Chairman Engel of the Foreign Affairs Committee were able to negotiate witnesses and documents, while Democrats in the Judiciary Committee cried that the administration was stonewalling them. Chairman Nadler was, in fact, the obstruction agent in our committee even with us in the minority. I had sent eight letters to Chairman Nadler asking that he answer my questions regarding the procedures that we would be following in the committee. Only one of those was ever answered, and that was about my witness list, which was just summarily denied. When you do not even answer requests, much less grant them, you are the instrument of obstruction. The chairman kept repeating that the administration said that it would fight all subpoenas related to the impeachment. I would like to remind everyone that this statement was made in April almost six months before the impeachment article HR 660 was passed. When we would bring up that the court was the entity for these disputes to be adjudicated, the Democrats would just say that time was of the essence and they could not wait. Notice this in the face of saying that the president was obstructing Congress while at the same time not taking advantage of the very resources that are at Congress's reach. If this were not so important, it would just be sad. The facts do bear this complaint out either.

The accusation by the Democrats that the Trump administration had been completely uncooperative is false. Over time they had sent over forty-five witnesses to both the Judiciary and House Oversight Committees and had supplied over 100,000 pages of documents to the Oversight Committee. The administration had cooperated in the investigations into the White House security clearance process and the investigations at the border, even allowing and accommodating nine surprise congressional visits in August and September of 2019. It also supplied over 9,600 documents in response to the issue of child separations at the border. The administration set up observation for committee staff at thirteen ICE detention facilities, more than ten Customs and Border Patrol holding facilities, and six state-licensed privately run facilities that were under federal contract. And high-level leaders of these agencies had testified before Congress. The administration had attempted to work with this Democrats in Congress. The problem was that Democrats believed that nothing was off limits. It is not unusual for presidents and their counsel to deny access or withhold information that would be considered privileged information. It happened under President Clinton, President Bush, and President Obama. In fact, it even happened all the way back to our first president, George Washington.

I am now convinced that the administration's perceived withholding was not the problem. Congress has dealt with this since its founding. The problem was twofold: they did not have much time, and they believed that the president should just give them everything, no matter the reason, because they were convinced that he was guilty and they did not want to have to wait on the things they thought would help them. The whole system was turned upside down.

In the end, it was never in doubt that the articles would be voted out of committee. But as I sat there watching history transpire, I was saddened that the Democrats would say anything to make their case. One lie was that the delay in the money was costing lives in Ukraine. This was an easy lie to debunk because even the Office of Management and Budget said the money was for future use, not current needs. You would have thought that once confronted with the truth, they would have backed off. You would be mistaken. During the markup, a member on the Democratic side brought this up early. We presented evidence that it was not true and thought that was the end of it. We were wrong. When Congressman Eric Swalwell (D-CA), in his over-the-top manner, spewed the lie again, I had had all I could take. As someone who has served in a war zone and seen real death from the battlefield up close, I could not let this lie stand. I spoke of how disgusting it was to repeat an argument that he knew was a lie to evoke emotion against the administration, to imply they had gotten people killed. It was so below the decorum of our committee, but I had begun to expect most anything. The chairman did not even speak up to try and stop it. I sat right next to him and showed him to the proof of the inaccuracy, but all he did was shrug and give a slight annoyed grin. The process was atrocious, but they had a job to do, and he would complete it.

As the committee dragged on, I was surprised at how much the Democrats kept arguing our members' amendments. It should be noted that the one thing that Democrats had was the numbers to pass the articles. Timing was up to them, but as the day dragged on, they just kept trying to argue the amendments. It still to this day surprises me that the chairman and other members of their staffs did not encourage their members to talk less and move to vote the amendments down quickly. The ones caught in this unexpectedly were the spouses like mine or the committee members who had come up for the White House Christmas party. As the day dragged on later and later, my wife and many of the others went and got changed thinking that we might be done in time to go. Martha Roby, congresswoman from Alabama, had her young son up so he could go to the White House with her. You could see the disappointment spread as the hearing continued. At one point I went out and sat with my bride as she sat there dressed up, waiting to go to the party. Unfortunately, that would not happen, and she had a plane to catch that night to get back to school the next day. I was able to make arrangements for the next day for members and family who were still in town to take them to the White House for a West Wing tour and a chance to see the president.

The ending of the meeting that day was probably one of the lowest times I had in Congress. As the evening wore on, we began to talk with the Democratic staff and the chairman about how many more amendments we had and how much longer we would go. They were mad that they had missed the prime-time news hour in which to end the hearings and proclaim to the world they had approved the articles of impeachment. So, at about 10:00 p.m., we reached an agreement that we were offering our last amendment and we were done. This meant that we could vote on the articles and get them sent to the floor. I thought that was the plan and had assurances that this was agreed upon and even had their staffs sign off on the plan. Then as we finished the amendment, the chairman decided to take a short recess. I should have known something was up, but even I could not see what was coming.

When the chairman sat back down, I knew something was wrong. He would not talk to me or even look at me. I believe that he was ashamed of what he was doing, and Jerry Nadler has a terrible poker face. He started reading a statement that said because of the gravity of the vote and its importance, he wanted everyone to go home, and we would reconvene in the morning to vote the articles out of committee. He then took the gavel as I was starting to speak and said the committee stood adjourned. I just lost it! I started yelling for the chairman to explain what was going on, and his staff just rushed him off the platform. It was proof of all the things we had been saying about these proceedings, that they were nothing more than a high-profile, partisan exercise designed to get the most attention they could to damage President Trump. I continued my rant in the committee room and then went to the press standup and continued to lay into the deep deception and sham the hearings had become.

I left the press conference and went and sat down in my office still shaking from anger. The issue was not that they decided to have the vote in the morning, but it was the deception in how they did it. They wanted to blindside us and make it look like they were being thoughtful before the vote. Anyone who had watched the proceedings knew that was not true; their minds had been made up for a long time. The thing that made me so angry was that even in our hardest moments that year on the committee, the chairman and the ranking member were able to come together to discuss and agree on things like adjourning or other issues that dealt with administration of the committee, not its actual work. This may seem small to the outside world, but when you are working on a committee that had been so dysfunctional, the only place you had to find common ground was that when you gave your word you kept it. That night the chairman, I believe, allowed his staff to convince him that he needed to hold the vote over and not tell us so we could not do anything or say anything about it. They just walked out on the platform and slapped us in the face and walked off. I lost so much respect for the chairman and his upper-level staff that night. If they had just given me a heads-up, I would not have liked it, but I would have understood their position. Instead, they went with a stunt that contributed to the distrust that I believe still lies in the halls of the Congress to this day. If you break your word, you have nothing left to trade upon.

The next day, I had a long conversation with Congressman Hakeem Jeffries (D-NY), with whom I had worked on many big pieces of legislation that became law. I told him how betrayed I and my staff felt. He agreed that it was a bad look but tried to put as good a spin on it as he could. Still, as I sat in the airport talking with him, I could feel in my spirit that this process had broken many things. It had broken the rules, it had shredded the concept of fairness, and now unfortunately, it had broken the one thing we still thought we had: honesty between the leadership of the committee and the rest of us. I got on the plane with a heavy heart, and as I sat down in the seat for the short flight back to Atlanta, I felt my body just crash, and I did something I do not normally do on these flights—I went to sleep. I had had all I could take for that week and was exhausted, but I knew that we still had a little more left to go.

I went home knowing that when I got on that plane again, it would be to go back to Washington to end the House's part in the sham impeachment. The articles of impeachment would then go to Senate, and we knew that the Senate would not vote to remove the president. The sordid affair would come to an end, and the only thing that had been accomplished was that the Democrats had spent a whole year searching desperately for a way to impeach the president, and when they did, they could not even put a specific charge in the document. Instead, they spouted generalizations that would allow them to spin any story necessary for their members to try and explain to voters why they voted to impeach the president. Such a waste of time and effort. It still amazes me to this day how hatred for an individual allowed you to forfeit so much of your governing ability. Still, this was the plan, and I lived it each day. The only two things that were left for the articles of impeachment were to go to the Rules Committee and then to the House floor for debate and vote.

In this year of adventure, there had been many firsts for me. I called out Speaker Pelosi when she defamed the president on the floor, which meant she should have not been able to speak the rest of the day on the floor. But instead of accepting what she did was wrong as ruled by the House parliamentarian, she chose to have her punishment overturned by forcing her members to come to the House floor to vote to take away her punishment for breaking the rules and decorum of the House. In her mind, because she was the Speaker she could do whatever she wanted. And now I would go before the Rules Committee, a committee I served on for four years, to talk about the articles for the last time before they went to the House floor. Going to the Rules Committee is not unusual, but it was the first time that committee had handled an impeachment. In past impeachments, the rules were handled by unanimous consent. This meant that both parties found that the issue before them had merit and on things like procedure they could find common ground on how to proceed no matter whether or not they agreed with the articles. However, this was such a sham and was so blatantly partisan they could not get our side to even agree to the simple format rules that were needed to get the bill to the floor. They had to force it through by the power of the majority. So here we go with an appointment for a new first in the Rules Committee.

The Rules Committee has a partisan advantage for the majority of nine votes to four. The majority does not lose in the Rules Committee; they are there to keep the train running and listen to the bills or, in this case the articles of impeachment, and decide how the House would be able to debate or even amend certain bills. I could assure you this would be what is known as a closed rule, meaning no amendments would be allowed. The other thing that the Rules Committee has become is a place for the bill to be discussed ad nauseum. It is as close to a debating club that we have in the House. I had one rule when I testified before the Rules Committee and that was to answer what I wanted to and to share my point of view, but I was not going to entertain hypotheticals or chase the perpetual rabbits that members of the other party throw at you. Typically, the chairman and the ranking member are the two who initially present their sides on the pieces of legislation to the committee. After that it is open to any member to come and speak.

On this day when I arrived, I found out that it would not be me and Chairman Nadler, who had a family emergency, but me and Congressman Jamie Raskin of Maryland. I liked Jamie as a member, but he and I differed on most points that came before the body. He was a skilled debater and a worthy opponent in this room of one-sided ideas, and for eight hours that day we became the only members who testified before a committee of any kind about the articles before us. As we got ready to begin, a thought passed over me. The two people who have been pushing this impeachment the hardest never had to sit down and answer hostile questions about the issue before us. Neither Chairman Nadler, due to a family health issue, nor Chairman Schiff, who stayed in hidden in the basement somewhere, would be there to take questions and accountability for what we were doing. It just shows why the level of trust in Congress is at such an incredibly low level. In the end, except for lasting all day, the Rules Committee meeting was a formality that laid the table for the floor. The story in the House was coming to an end, and the cloud that I spoke of descending on the House was now coming to its final closure.

CHAPTER 7:
ARTICLES OF IMPEACHMENT

On December 18, 2019, the articles of impeachment were finally brought to the floor. The day would start out with the vote on the rule, and then we were to proceed with debate on the articles themselves. I love the floor of the House of Representatives. The history lays heavy on every part. You can look to the dais and hear the echoes of FDR telling us that December 7, 1941, would be a date that will live in infamy. You hear the debates that shaped our country. The joys and pain of our great nation have played out on this very floor since the Civil War. We have heard the reports of wars and of our accomplishments, such as our landing on the moon, and we have experienced the fear of days like September 11, 2001. The debates on this grand floor have shaped almost every aspect of our great republic. Every time I walk on the floor, I am reminded that this country is a place in which dreams can be had and that even a trooper's kid from North Georgia could have the opportunity to serve and represent his neighbors. However, on this day, I was both reflecting on what the day would entail and what would they say about us in the pages of history. Would they look back and see a body that was experiencing a short turn against its better nature, or was this the beginning of a partisan turn that in the end will only hurt the people we are elected to serve? I had said just a few weeks earlier on this floor that I could feel a dark cloud descending on the House, and, unfortunately, I was here to see it fall. I knew that nothing said today was going to change the result. We would leave today with the House voting to impeach President Trump just because they could.

It was also a day of sadness for me. I was not sad because I thought there was a wrongdoing that caused us to be here. No, the wrongdoing was our own. It was the belief that political outcomes were more important than having facts or crimes you could prove. So as the galleries started filling with members of the press, who normally sit anywhere else to casually pay attention to what goes on during the floor debate, the final act of the show that started almost twelve months ago would strut and fret for its final hours on stage.

The Speaker started it off with a discussion of the Pledge of Allegiance to our flag. She spoke of how we were a republic if we could keep it. Then she got to the part that caused me to cringe, as if someone had run their fingernails over a chalkboard. She said that she opened these proceedings to impeach President Donald Trump sadly and solemnly. She hid behind this talk of oath and duty, but I could only wonder to myself where the honor was if you had to trash the very body you lead to get the desired results you seek.

Steny Hoyer, the majority leader of the House, got up later and, continuing with the same calloused thought, said, "What I will do is remind Americans that the House provided President Trump every opportunity to prove his innocence." Read that statement again. Do you see what he has done? He stated that the president had every opportunity to prove his innocence. I could hear the leaders in our country who had served in the people's house groan from beyond the grave when, in one sentence, the majority leader of the House turned on its head the very principle that has made this country great and protected its citizens from the tyranny of the government. In this country, we start from the assumption that you are innocent. It is not the person accused who needs to prove anything. Instead, the one bringing the accusation bears that burden. If the leader of the Democrats was willing to admit to turning our sacred principles on their head, then nothing we said today would, in the end, matter.

The day played out as I expected. The only difficult thing for me that day was to try and keep track of everyone who wanted to speak on our side. I could not have done that without Ella Yates and Ericka Barker, who kept the lineup running and everyone on the floor when they were supposed to be. Jon Ferro, Bobby Parham, and Ashley Callen helped maintain the responses that I would lob back at the Democrats as they waged a never-ending battle to distort or embellish the truth. The biggest embellishment was the continual accusation of actual criminal acts that the president supposedly had been involved with. The problem with this argument was that if they had evidence of actual crimes, they would have included those in the articles. Instead, they were left with the ambiguous charges of abuse of power and obstruction of Congress. I was surprised that even Jerry Nadler and Adam Schiff did not try to come up with any new angles to put into the mix. Of course, there was no love lost between Adam Schiff and Jerry Nadler. Schiff had outmaneuvered Nadler all year, and when it came time for the final push to impeach, it was Adam Schiff calling the shots and then letting the Judiciary Committee take the blame for the weak articles of impeachment.

On our side, we made the best of our few minutes of time to score some wonderful points. Congressman Mark Meadows had one of the better lines when he talked about how that, with all the talk about the Constitution, he had never seen so many Constitutional originalists on the Democratic side of the aisle; but he quickly reminded them that this impeachment was not about the Constitution but about power. The minority leader for the Republicans, Kevin McCarthy, closed out our side with a fiery reminder that this was not just a three-month affair but a three-year affair, with many of the Democrats saying they want-ed to impeach Donald Trump long before the impeachment process ever started. They had just been just looking for an excuse. Over and over, our members took to the floor to decry what was happening and remind America that while they were working hard every day to make their own lives better, the Democrats in Congress were simply trying to find ways to get rid of a president they did not like.

When it was time for me to bring our arguments to a close right before Leader McCarthy spoke, I felt a rush of adrenaline. This was the last opportunity I had to frame this debate before we took that final vote. I find it interesting that the Democrats would even talk about fairness on this day. You see, as I have gone back over the events of that year and laid them out, I am more convinced than ever that there was NO factual basis for the impeachment of Donald Trump. Yet as bad as that was, the damage that will last the longest is the treatment of the rules of the House to get the intended result. It was this thought that I tried to convey to the House when I rose to speak that evening. By this time, the House floor was full of members, the gallery was full of press, and we had even gotten word that the president, who was about to do a rally in Milwaukee, was waiting before he spoke so he could watch the proceedings on the floor as they played out. It was a bit intimidating to get up and speak, but the words came easily. I had lived this for the past three years and up close for the past year. I spoke of the cloud that was descending and laid out the case for why the Democrats were wrong. The problem, I concluded, was not about punishing someone for doing something wrong; it was about enacting political retribution on someone they never thought would win. They were merely trying to make sure that he would never win again.

Before I began my speech, I sat at the desk on the floor and thought about what I should say. I really wanted to say something about not just the treachery that the Democrats had pulled, but also where I saw us going when this ugly episode was finally behind us. I wanted to look beyond the moment and let the world know that this was not the end and that we as a House were better than this. This is what I said:

> *Right now the dark cloud is descending upon this House. I am fearful, Madam Speaker, when I look out into that abyss. I don't know what I see, but I'll tell you what I do see. I see a president who will put his head down, even through this sham impeachment, and he will do his job. He will put the American people first. He will tell them, I care about you. He will still put the economy first, and he will make sure that this country stands strong. That is what I see in this abyss. That is where we are going.*

When I was through, our side was on their feet cheering. I felt like I had accomplished, at least for a moment, the goal of reminding those of us who had struggled with the events of this past year that we would overcome. We would live to see a better day. That year taught me one thing: if you are willing to destroy the institution that you serve for political or momentary gain, you will lose far more than you ever set out to gain. The House suffered a lot over that year from an abusive process, but the sun did come back up again the next day. And it is within all our power to learn the lesson that the clock and the calendar are cruel taskmasters.

EPILOGUE

The Democrats in the House finished their push against the clock and calendar in the House and sent the articles of impeachment to the Senate in January 2020. Speaker Pelosi held the transmission of the articles, trying to hold out for an agreement with the Senate to have what she deemed was a "fair trial." The irony of that hung heavy against the backdrop of the farce that had taken place in the House. She now wanted the Senate to do what she refused to do. However, as I and others had warned the trial in the Senate went nowhere and only one Republican, Mitt Romney, voted for impeaching President Trump on one of the articles. In the end the curtain came down and the only thing that was lasting was the damage done to the institution of Congress willfully carried out by Speaker Pelosi and the Democratic majority in the House.

In January, after the impeachment trial, in which I served as an advisor to the president's legal team, I decided to not run for reelection to the House and instead launched a run for the US Senate from Georgia. Everywhere I went that year during the campaign, I would always have people who would come up and want to talk about the impeachment and the events surrounding it. I was amazed that even Democrats who would never have voted for me would say that in the end the proceedings were not about finding a real crime as much as it was to damage President Trump going into the next election cycle. Although my race for the Senate did not end with a victory, I could see that the fight that we had put up defending not only the integrity of the House of Representatives but President Trump mattered to those who watched it unfold.

In the end, the only real lasting effect of the impeachment was what I feared most. That the tyranny of the majority, and its reckless abuse of power would lead to not only distrust by the American people but a breakdown of any modicum of civility in the House of Representatives. The other outcome of this is that impeachment came to be viewed as just another political tool to get back at an administration that the majority did not like. This was best exemplified by the fact that the Democrats who impeached President Trump again raced the clock and the calendar in January 2021 in the aftermath of the overrunning of the Capitol on January 6. This time, after already setting the precedent that the rules did not matter, the House impeached the president with less than a month left in his term—without even holding a single hearing! Of course, when you have showed no concern for the rules the first time it gets easier the next time.

In the end, the events of the past few years have led to what I fear most: an institution that should be about the highest ideals and debate has been reduced to a partisan struggle in which the only goal is to win no matter the cost. The clock and the calendar are cruel taskmasters and when you are in a race against them you rarely notice that the corners you cut now will have long-lasting effects even after your quest is through. I can only hope that now as we look back, we can see the effects and determine that the American people deserve better but more importantly our democracy deserves better. If we do not, then we let the abnormal become the normal—and we are better than that.